W9-BVW-379

XRX BOOKS

the Best of Knitter's

ARANS
CELTICS

The Best of Knitter's ARANS & CELTICS
PUBLISHED BY XRX BOOKS

PUBLISHER
Alexis Yiorgos Xenakis

EDITOR
Elaine Rowley

MANAGING EDITOR
David Xenakis

EDITORIAL ASSISTANT
Sue Nelson

INSTRUCTION EDITORS
Joni Coniglio
Gail McHugh

INSTRUCTION ASSISTANTS
Mary Lou Eastman
Ingrid Reed

COPY EDITOR
Holly Brunner

GRAPHIC DESIGNER
Bob Natz

PHOTOGRAPHER
Alexis Yiorgos Xenakis

PRODUCTION DIRECTOR
DIGITAL COLOR SPECIALIST
Dennis Pearson

PRODUCTION CHIEF
TECHNICAL ILLUSTRATOR
Carol Skallerud

BOOK PRODUCTION MANAGER
Nancy Steers

DIGITAL PREPRESS
Everett Baker

TECHNICAL ILLUSTRATIONS
Jay Reeve

FIRST PUBLISHED IN USA
IN 2003 BY XRX, INC.

COPYRIGHT © 2003 XRX, INC.

ISBN 1-8937620-5-X

Produced by XRX, Inc.
PO Box 1525
Sioux Falls, SD 57101-1525
605.338.2450

visit us online at
www.knittinguniverse.com

Knitter's K16

Knitter's K44

Knitter's K40

Knitter's K46

Rediscover our cabled past!

The Best of Knitter's: Arans & Celtics includes reader's favorites from eight issues of Knitter's Magazine.

Although no longer available in their original form, these classics are once again yours for the knitting.

Knitter's K48

Knitter's K51

Knitter's K56

Knitter's K60

contents

pullovers

Bulky wool makes even the simplest knitting stand out in bold relief. Easy-to-knit ribs become thick, twisted ropes, to contrast with the smooth, flat cable at the center front of the sweater.

Deborah Newton

twisted knotwork

Back

With larger needles, cast on 65 (73, 79) sts. *Begin Charts A and B: Row 1* (RS) K2, p2 (0, 3), work Chart A over 24 (30, 30) sts, 9 sts Chart B, Chart A over 24 (30, 30) sts, p2 (0, 3), k2. *Row 2* P2, k2 (0, 3), Chart A over 24 (30, 30) sts, 9 sts Chart B, Chart A over 24 (30, 30) sts, k2 (0, 3), p2. Continue in pats as established until piece measures 21 (22, 23)" from beginning, end with a WS row.

Shape shoulders and neck

Mark center 7 (9, 9) sts. Bind off 7 (8, 9) sts at beginning of next 6 rows for shoulders, AT SAME TIME, join a 2nd ball of yarn at neck edge and bind off center 7 (9, 9) sts. Working both sides at same time with separate balls of yarn, bind off from each neck edge 4 sts twice.

Front

Work as for back until piece measures 19 (20, 21)" from beginning, end with a WS row.

Shape neck and shoulders

Next row (RS) Work 29 (32, 35) sts, join 2nd ball of yarn, bind off center 7 (9, 9) sts, work to end. Working both sides at same time with separate balls of yarn, bind off from each neck edge 2 sts 4 times—21 (24, 27) sts each side. Work even until piece measures same length as back to shoulder, end with a WS row.

Shape shoulders

Bind off from each shoulder edge 7 (8, 9) sts 3 times.

Sleeves

With smaller needles, cast on 32 (32, 40) sts. Work Chart C for 3", ending with

chart row 1. *Next row* (WS) Purl, inc 2 (2, 0) sts evenly across—34 (34, 40) sts. Change to larger needles. *Next row* (RS) K2, work Chart A over center 30 (30, 36) sts, k2. Continue in pat as established, inc 1 st each side (working incs into Chart A pat inside 2 selvage sts each side) every 4th row 9 times, then every 6th row 2 (4, 4) times—56 (60, 66) sts. Work even until piece measures 17 (18, 18)" from beginning. Bind off.

Finishing

Sew shoulders.

Neckband

With RS facing and circular needle, pick up and k56 (64, 64) sts evenly around neck edge. Place marker and join. Work Chart C in rounds for 4½". Bind off. Place markers 9 (10, 11)" down from shoulders on front and back for armholes. Sew top of sleeves between markers. Sew side and sleeve seams. ∩

Skill Easy+
Fit Oversized
Sizes S (M, L). Shown in Medium.
Finished measurements 44 (48, 52)" around and 23 (24, 25)" long.
Gauge 10 sts and 14 rows to 10cm/4" over St st (k on RS, p on WS), using larger needles; 12 sts and 14 rows to 10cm/4" over Chart A.
Yarns 760 (860, 970) yds. Super bulky weight.
Needles Sizes 8 and 9mm/US 11 and 13, *or size to obtain gauge.*
Size 8mm/US 11 circular, 40cm/16" long.
Extras Cable needle (cn).
Original yarn Reynolds Bulky Lopi (100% wool; 3½oz/100g; 66 yds/60m).

□ K on RS, p on WS
▨ P on RS, k on WS

 1/1 RT K2tog and leave sts on needle, insert RH needle between 2 sts just knit, and knit the first st; sl both sts off needle.

2/2 RC Sl 2 to cn, hold to back, k2; k2 from cn.

2/2 LC Sl 2 to cn, hold to front, k2; k2 from cn.

Chart A

6-st rep

Chart B

9 sts

Chart C

8-st rep

Front/Back Pat Arrangement

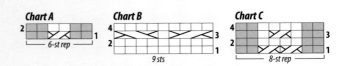

2 sts St st	2 (0, 3) sts Rev St st	24 (30, 30) sts Chart A	Chart B	24 (30, 30) sts Chart A	2 (0, 3) sts Rev St st	2 sts St st

5

I actually designed this knitting pattern years ago. I first designed a pattern with only the 'woven strips' and seed stitch block in between. Later I added one cable twist to the woven strip, and then another. This design is easy to adjust size-wise and yarn-wise, since you can simply knit more or less of the seed stitch pattern between the vertical woven strips. The shaping is simple, the design is great fun to knit, and the yarn makes this a classic you'll want to wear for years.

Nancy Marchant

wondrous woven cables

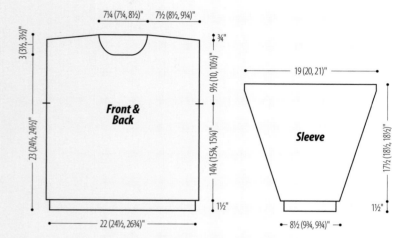

Back

With smaller needles, cast on 111 (123, 135) sts. **Begin K3, P3 Rib: Row 1** (RS) *K3, p3; rep from*, end k3. Continue in rib pat until piece measures 1½", inc 5 sts evenly across last (WS) row—116 (128, 140) sts. Change to larger needles. **Begin Chart pat: Row 1** (RS) Beginning as indicated for back, work to end of 29-st rep, then work rep 3 times more, end chart as indicated. Continue in pat as established through chart row 37, then rep rows 6–37 until piece measures 25 (27¼, 27¼)" from beginning, end with a WS row.

Shape shoulders

Bind off 13 (15, 16) sts at beginning of next 6 rows. Bind off remaining 38 (38, 44) sts.

Front

Work as for back until piece measures 23 (24½, 24½)" from beginning, end with a WS row.

Shape neck

Next row (RS) Continue pats, work 52 (58, 61) sts, join 2nd ball of yarn and bind off center 12 (12, 18) sts, work to end. Working both sides at same time, bind off from each neck edge 3 sts once, 2 sts 3 times, 1 st 4 times. When same length as back to shoulder, shape shoulder as for back.

Sleeves

With smaller needles, cast on 45 (51, 51) sts. Work 1½" in K3, P3 rib, end with a WS row. Change to larger needles. **Begin Chart pat: Row 1** (RS) Begin as indicated for sleeve, work chart pat across, end as indicated. Continue in chart pat as established, AT SAME TIME, inc 1 st each side (working incs into seed st and horizontal pat only) on 5th row, then every 4th row 21 (17, 26) times more, every 6th row 5 (9, 3) times—99 (105, 111) sts. Work even until piece measures 19 (20, 20)" from beginning. Bind off.

Finishing

Block pieces. Sew shoulders.

Neckband

With RS facing and circular needle, begin at left shoulder and pick up and k46 (52, 58) sts evenly along front neck, 38 (38, 44) sts along back neck—84 (90, 102) sts. Place marker, join and work 2" in K3, P3 rib. Bind off. Fold neckband in half to WS and sew in place. Place markers 9½ (10, 10½)" down from shoulders on front and back for armhole. Sew top of sleeves between markers. Sew side and sleeve seams. ∩

Skill Intermediate

Fit Loose

Sizes S (M, L). Shown in Medium.

Finished measurements 44 (49, 53½)" around and 26 (28, 28)" long.

Gauge 21 sts and 29 rows equal 10cm/4" over Chart pat, using larger needles.

Yarn 1360 (1600, 1720) yds. Medium weight.

Needles Sizes 3.5 and 4mm/US 4 and 6, *or size to obtain gauge.*

Size 3.5mm/US 4 circular needle, 40cm/16" long.

Extras Cable needle (cn). Stitch markers.

Original yarn Harrisville Highland Style (100% wool; 3½oz/100g; 200yds/180m).

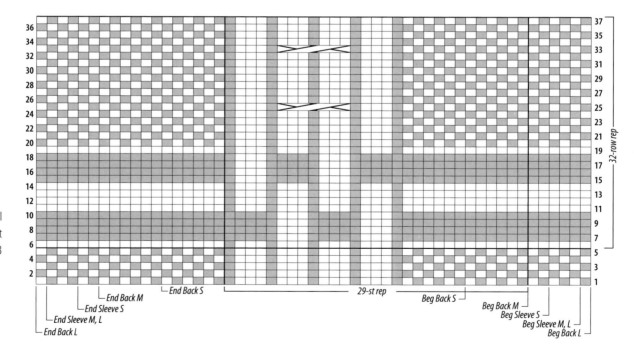

K on RS, p on WS

P on RS, k on WS

3/1/3 RC Sl 4 to cn, hold to back, k3; sl last st from cn to LH needle and purl it; k3 from cn.

End Back S

End Back M

End Sleeve S

End Sleeve M, L

End Back L

29-st rep

Beg Back S

Beg Back M

Beg Sleeve S

Beg Sleeve M, L

Beg Back L

32-row rep

wondrous woven cables

Bebenhausen windows

I lived in Stuttgart, Germany, near the Black Forest, for two years. A few kilometers south was the tiny town of Bebenhausen. I often visited its Cistercian monastery, which dates from 1190. Although the monks live austere lives, their chapels and cloister are decorated in a Celtic celebration of plants, zoomorphic animals, and knotwork. Even the wooden pillars supporting the roofs have marvelous cable designs snaking up them. The wrought iron tracery on the windows of the cloister inspired this sweater.

Sue Mink

Bebenhausen windows

Notes

1 Work chart for size you are making. **2** For body, work rep of Chart A circularly to underarm, then divide sts in half and work Chart B back and forth in rows (adding 1 selvage st each side) for front and back. **3** For sleeve, work all 25 (27, 29) sts of Chart A, decreasing 1 st on row 25 (27, 29).

Body

With smaller 29" needle, cast on 210 (230, 250) sts. Being careful not to twist sts, place marker (pm) and join. *Begin Chart A: Rnd 1* Work 21-st rep (23-st rep, 25-st rep) 10 times. Continue in pat through chart rnd 12. Change to larger needle. Work through chart rnd 30 (32, 34)—200 (220, 240) sts. Rep rnds 27–30 (29–32, 31–34) until piece measures approx 14½ (15½, 16½)" from beginning, end with chart rnd 30 (32, 34).

Divide for front and back

Begin Chart B: Row 1 (RS) Work 20-st rep (22-st rep, 24-st rep) of Chart B 5 times (for back), then place rem 100 (110, 120) sts on hold for front. Turn and work back and forth in rows as follows: Work chart row 2 across, inc 1 st at each side (for selvage sts)—102 (112, 122) sts. Keeping 1 st at each side in garter st (k every row), continue in chart pat through row 24 (30, 32), then rep rows 9–24 (11–30, 9–32) until armhole measures 9 (9, 9½)", end with a WS row.

Shape neck

Next row (RS) Continue pat, work 41 (46, 50) sts, join a 2nd ball of yarn and bind off center 20 (20, 22) sts, work to end. Working both sides at same time, bind off from each neck edge 3 sts twice—35 (40, 44) sts each side. Work even until armhole measures 10 (10, 10½)". Bind off all sts.

Front

With RS facing, join yarn at underarm and work as for back until armhole measures 7½", end with a WS row.

Shape neck

Next row (RS) Work 44 (49, 53) sts, join 2nd ball of yarn and bind off center 14 (14, 16) sts, work to end. Working both sides at same time, bind off from each neck edge 3 sts once, 2 sts 3 times—35 (40, 44) sts each side. Work even until armhole measures same length as back to shoulder. Bind off all sts.

Sleeves

With smaller 29" needle, cast on 45 (47, 49) sts. Work back and forth in rows as follows: *Begin Chart A: Row 1* (RS) [K1, p1] 5 times, work Chart A over 25 (27, 29) sts, [p1, k1] 5 times. *Row 2* K2, [p1, k1] 4 times, work Chart A over 25 (27, 29) sts, [k1, p1] 4 times, k2. Work pats as established through row 12. Change to larger needle. *Next row* (RS) K1, p9, work chart pat over 25 (27, 29) sts, p9, k1. *Next row* (WS) K10, work chart pat over 25 (27, 29) sts, k10. Continue in pats as established, AT SAME TIME, inc 1 st each side (working incs into rev St st inside selvage sts each side) on next row, then every other row 15 times more—76 (78, 80) sts. Work even until sleeve measures 18½ (19, 20)" from beginning. Bind off all sts.

Finishing

Block pieces. Sew shoulders.

Neckband

With RS facing and 16" needle, begin at left shoulder and pick up and k 66 (66, 70) sts evenly around neck edge. Pm, join and work in rnds of k1, p1 rib for 5". Fold to WS and sew sts to first row. Centering middle cable on shoulder seams, sew top of sleeves to armholes. Sew sleeve seams. ∩

Skill Intermediate
Fit Loose
Sizes S (M, L). Shown in Medium.
Finished measurements 40 (44, 48½)" around and 24½ (25½, 27)" long.
Gauge 15 sts and 18 rows equal 10cm/4" over St st (k on RS, p on WS), using larger needles.
Yarn 1030 (1140, 1310) yds. Bulky weight.
Needles Size 4.5 and 5.5mm/US7 and 9 circular needles, 72cm/29" long, *or size to obtain gauge.* Size 4.5mm/US7 circular needle, 40cm/16" long.
Extras Cable needle (cn). Stitch markers.
Original yarn Classic Elite Montera (50% llama, 50% wool; 3½oz/100g; 127 yds/114m).

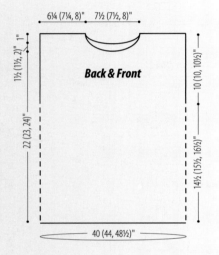

Back & Front

6¼ (7¼, 8)"   7½ (7½, 8)"

1½ (1½, 2)"   1"

10 (10, 10½)"

22 (23, 24)"

14½ (15½, 16½)"

40 (44, 48½)"

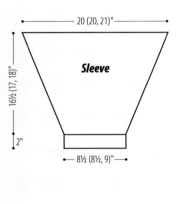

Sleeve

20 (20, 21)"

16½ (17, 18)"

2"

8½ (8½, 9)"

Chart A (Size L)

Chart for Sleeve (worked back and forth)
Chart for Body (worked circularly)

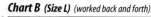

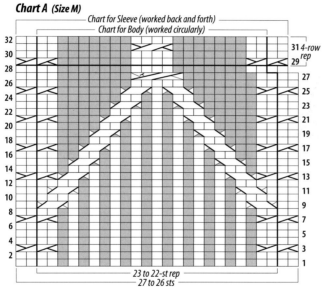

34 32 30 28 26 24 22 20 18 16 14 12 10 8 6 4 2

33 4-row rep
31
29 27 25 23 21 19 17 15 13 11 9 7 5 3 1

25 to 24-st rep
29 to 28 sts

CHART B NOTE On chart rows that begin with partial cables, work first 2 sts at beginning of first repeat and last 2 sts of last repeat in St st.

Chart B (Size L) (worked back and forth)

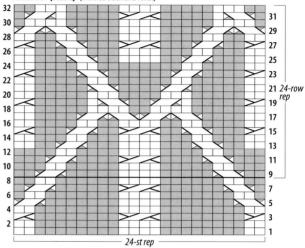

32 30 28 26 24 22 20 18 16 14 12 10 8 6 4 2

31 29 27 25 23 21 24-row rep
19 17 15 13 11 9 7 5 3 1

24-st rep

Key

- ☐ K on RS, p on WS
- ▨ P on RS, k on WS
- ⟋ **2/1 RC** Sl 1 to cn, hold to back, k2; k1 from cn.
- ⟍ **2/1 LC** Sl 2 to cn, hold to front, k1; k2 from cn.
- ⟋ **2/1 RPC** Sl 1 to cn, hold to back, k2; p1 from cn.
- ⟍ **2/1 LPC** Sl 2 to cn, hold to front, p1; k2 from cn.
- ⟋ **2/2 RC** Sl 2 to cn, hold to back, k2; k2 from cn.
- ⟋ **2/3 RC DEC** Sl 3 to cn, hold to back, k2; k2tog, k1 from cn (1 st dec).

Chart A (Size M)

Chart for Sleeve (worked back and forth)
Chart for Body (worked circularly)

32 30 28 26 24 22 20 18 16 14 12 10 8 6 4 2

31 4-row rep
29 27 25 23 21 19 17 15 13 11 9 7 5 3 1

23 to 22-st rep
27 to 26 sts

Chart B (Size M) (worked back and forth)

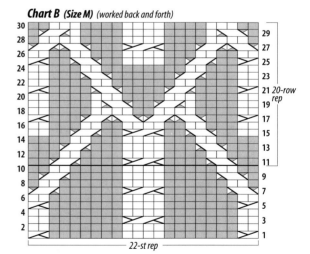

30 28 26 24 22 20 18 16 14 12 10 8 6 4 2

29 27 25 23 21 20-row rep
19 17 15 13 11 9 7 5 3 1

22-st rep

Chart A (Size S)

Chart for Sleeve (worked back and forth)
Chart for Body (worked circularly)

30 28 26 24 22 20 18 16 14 12 10 8 6 4 2

29 4-row rep
27 25 23 21 19 17 15 13 11 9 7 5 3 1

21 to 20-st rep
25 to 24 sts

Chart B (Size S) (worked back and forth)

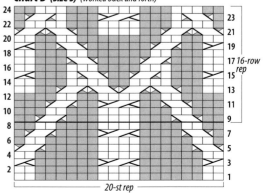

24 22 20 18 16 14 12 10 8 6 4 2

23 21 19 17 16-row rep
15 13 11 9 7 5 3 1

20-st rep

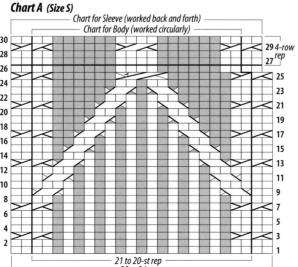

There is no doubt that both the process and the product are rewarding in this Aran. The traditional circular construction, square armholes, and use of steeks is given flair with a short, boxy shape, an interesting combination of pattern stitches, a slightly deeper crew neck, and removable knitted shoulder pads. The body stitch patterns are the same front and back; the sleeves are complementary to, but different from the body. No boredom here! You are sure to learn something new in the course of this project—I did.

Rosemary Martin

abbreviated Aran

Notes

1 See *School*, p. 102, for M1P, ssk, wrapping sts for short rows, loop cast-on, and 3-needle bind-off. **2** Sweater is worked in rnds using steeks at armholes and neck. **3** Shoulders are worked in rows.

1/1 RT Knit 2nd st on LH needle, then knit first st slipping both sts from needle.

Body

With smaller 24" needle, cast on 188 (208, 228) sts. Place rnd marker (pm) and join, being careful not to twist sts. Work in k2, p2 rib for 1½", inc 10 (12, 14) sts evenly on last rnd—198 (220, 242) sts. Change to larger needle. *Begin Charts:* **Rnd 1** *P 0 (0, 4), 1/1 RT 0 (0, 1) time, p7 (9, 9), 1/1 RT, work Chart A over 18 sts, 1/1 RT, work Chart B over 8 (10, 10) sts, 1/1 RT, work Chart C over 20 (22, 22) sts, 1/1 RT, work Chart B over 8 (10, 10) sts, 1/1 RT, work Chart A over 18 sts, 1/1 RT, p8 (9, 9), 1/1 RT 0 (1, 1) time, p0 (0, 5); pm and rep from *. Continue in pat as est until rnd 14 (18, 18) of Chart A has been completed twice, piece measures approx 8½ (9, 9)" from beginning.

Shape armholes

Note Steeks are started here. The steek sts are not included in any body st counts. Steek sts should be worked in St st.

Next rnd *Work to 8 (11, 13) sts before marker, place next 15 (20, 25) sts on hold removing marker, using loop cast-on, cast on 5 sts for steek onto RH needle; rep from *, pm—84 (90, 96) sts each on front and back. Continue in est pat, work 26 (30, 38) rnds, ending with rnd 13 (21, 1) of Chart A, piece measures approx 4½ (5¼, 6½)" from beginning of armhole.

Shape front neck

Note Neck decs are made each side of the center steek.

Next rnd Work 27 (28, 31) sts, place center 30 (34, 34) st on hold, using loop cast-on, cast on 3 sts on RH needle and work to end.

Next (dec) rnd Work to 2 sts before steek, p2tog, k3 steek sts, p2tog, work to end. Rep dec rnd every other rnd 3 times more—23 (24, 27) sts each side of neck. Work 16 rnds ending with rnd 9 (17, 25) of Chart A. Armhole measures approx 8½ (9¼, 10½)".

Shape shoulders

Note Front and back are worked separately in rows.

Remove rnd marker and slip 5 steek sts of left armhole onto LH needle, then place 84 (90, 96) back sts and 5 steek sts of right armhole on hold.

Front

Begin short row shoulder charts Bind off 5 steek sts then continue with row 1

of shoulder chart for your size. Bind off center 3 steek sts on Chart row 5. Put sts on hold.

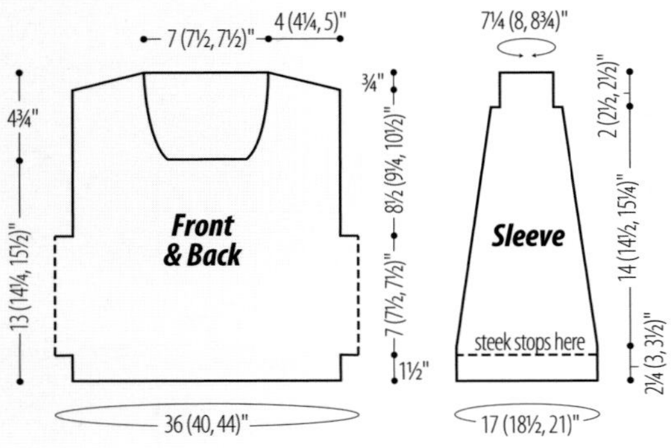

Back

Work as for front except work center 38 (42, 42) sts in pat instead of 3 steek sts. *Row 5: For Size S ONLY* Work knits and purls as they appear instead of pat across center 38 sts. *All Sizes* Put center 38 (42, 42) sts on hold after working them on row 5.

Sewing and cutting steeks

With RS facing and sewing machine set at a fairly wide zigzag and medium st length, stitch down the middle of the 2 sts on either side of center st of steeks. If done by hand use doubled sewing thread and make small back sts down center of same sts. Do this for each armhole and center of neck. Then, keeping hand underneath the steek, cut along the center st of steek from cast-on to bound-off edge. Join shoulders using 3-needle bind-off.

Sleeves

Note Sleeves are picked up at armhole and worked downward. A steek is used at the straight part at the top.

With RS facing and larger 16" needle, beginning at underarm and keeping steek sts flat, pick up between last pat st and first steek st 92 (100, 114) sts evenly along edges of armhole (leaving underarm sts on hold), pm, then cast-on 5 sts for steek. Join and work as follows: p0 (3, 10), 1/1 RT 0 (1, 1) time, p10 (9, 9), 1/1 RT, p9, 1/1 RT, work Chart D over 12 sts, 1/1 RT, work Chart E over 18 sts, 1/1 RT, work Chart D over 12 sts beginning with rnd 21, 1/1 RT, p9, 1/1 RT, p10 (9, 9), 1/1 RT 0 (1, 1) time, p0 (3, 10). Work 7 (10, 13) rnds more in est pat. **Next rnd** Remove marker, bind off 5 steek sts, work to end. Sew sts at either side of center steek st as before, but DO NOT cut the steek. **Next rnd** Join and work as follows: *Sizes S and L ONLY* K1, pm, work to 2 sts before marker, 1/1 RT. *Size M ONLY* Pm, p2, M1P, work to last

Skill Advanced
Fit Standard
Sizes S (M, L). Shown in Medium.
Finished measurements 36 (40, 44)" around and 17¾ (19, 20¼)" long.
Gauge 22 sts and 24 rnds equal 10cm/4" over Chart C, using larger needles.
Yarn 1310 (1540, 1780) yds. Medium weight.
Needles Sizes 3.75 and 4.5mm/US 5 and 7 circular needles, 40 and 60cm/16" and 24" long, *or size to obtain gauge.*
Four 3.75mm/US 5 double pointed (dpn).
Extras Stitch holders and markers; sewing machine or sewing needle; matching color sewing thread.
Original yarn Harrisville Trillium (50% cotton, 50% wool; 3½oz/100g; 440yds/400m).

Measurements on schematic: 7 (7½, 7½)" · 4 (4¼, 5)" · 7¼ (8, 8¾)" · ¾" · 4¾" · 13 (14¼, 15½)" · 7 (7½, 7½)" · 8½ (9¼, 10½)" · 1½" · 2 (2½, 2½)" · 14 (14½, 15¼)" · **Front & Back** · **Sleeve** · steek stops here · 2¼ (3, 3½)" · 36 (40, 44)" · 17 (18½, 21)"

3 sts, [p1, M1P] twice, p1—103 sts. **All Sizes** Work 3 rnds. **Note** For sizes S and L, decs are worked using the 3rd and 4th sts of rnd and last 2 sts of rnd, keeping the first 2 sts as 1/1 RT. For size M decs are worked using the 2nd and 3rd sts of the rnd and the last 2 sts of rnd, keeping the first st as a p. Use p2tog for decs except when 1/1 RTs converge, then for first dec use k2tog and for last dec use ssk keeping remaining k sts as knit until they become purls as part of pat.

Work decs at beginning and end of rnd as described on next rnd, then every 4th rnd 20 (21, 23) times more—50 (59, 66) sts. Work 3 (4, 1) rnd even, ending with rnd 1 (9, 1) of Chart E. Sleeve measures approx 16¼ (17½, 18¾)". Change to dpns. **Rnd 1** Work k2, p2 rib, dec 10 (15, 18) sts evenly around—40 (44, 48) sts. Work rib for 2 (2½, 2½)". Bind off in pat.

Finishing

Neckband

With RC facing and smaller 16" needle, beginning at right shoulder, work as follows: **For Size S ONLY** [K2, p2] 9 times, k2, pick up 18 sts along left neck steek edge as before, [k2, p2] 7 times, k2, pick up 18 sts along right neck steek edge—104 sts. **For Sizes M and L ONLY** [K2, p2] 3 times, *k2, p2tog, p1, k2, [p2tog] twice, k2, p2tog, p1, k2*, [p2, k2] 3 times, pick up 18 sts along left neck steek edge, [k2, p2] twice, work from * to * once, [p2, k2] twice, pick up 18 sts along right neck steek edge—104 sts. Pm, work k2, p2 rib for 1". Bind off in pat.

Underarms

Put sts from hold onto dpn. Cut steek. Graft half of open sts to pat edge of each steek (see How-to, p. 15).

Tack steeks to inside. Block. ∩

☐ K on RS, p on WS

☐ P on RS, k on WS

▨ P2tog

ⓦ Wrap st and turn work

▨ P into front and back of stitch

▨ **1/1 RT (On RS)** Knit 2nd st on LH needle, then knit first st slipping both sts from needle. **(On WS)** Purl 2nd st on LH needle, then purl first st slipping both sts from needle.

▨ **1/1 RPC** Sl 1 to cn, hold to back, k1; p1 from cn.

▨ **1/1 RPC TBL** Sl 1 to cn, hold to back, k1 through back loop (tbl); p1 from cn.

▨ **1/1 LPC TBL** Sl 1 to cn, hold to front, p1; k1tbl from cn.

▨ **2/1 RC** Sl 1 to cn, hold to back, k2; k1 from cn.

▨ **2/1 LC** Sl 2 to cn, hold to front, k1; k2 from cn.

▨ **2/1 RPC** Sl 1 to cn, hold to back, k2; p1 from cn.

▨ **2/1 LPC** Sl 2 to cn, hold to front, p1; k2 from cn.

▨ **2/2 RC** Sl 2 to cn, hold to back, k2; k2 from cn.

▨ **2/2 LC** Sl 2 to cn, hold to front, k2; k2 from cn.

▨ **3/3 LC** Sl 3 to cn, hold to front, k3; k3 from cn.

▨ **2/2/2 RIB RC** Sl 4 to cn, hold to front, k2, sl 2 p sts from cn to LH needle, move cn to back, p2; k2 from cn.

---

knitter's tips: border a future vest, pad a shoulder

VERTICAL BORDER

Aran patterns create beautiful vertical panels. So when my latest Aran vest was finished, I couldn't bring myself to pick up sts at the armhole and make the usual rib, which would form horizontal lines. Here's my solution: a way to make a vertical armhole rib and not detract from the overall effect. Have the underarm sts from the body on a holder, then with dpn cast on with invisible cast-on (see *School*, p. 102) half that number of sts. (This will be the width of the rib.) Work back and forth in k1, p1 rib on these sts, every other row slipping the first st on the armhole side and knitting the last st tog with a loop from the body. Continue up one side, across the shoulder and down the other side back to holder. Add the cast-on sts to the dpn, put sts from underarm holder on a dpn, turn RS tog and knit tog as you would for a 3-needle bind-off (see *School*). Although it started with a straight platform under the arm, this results in a flattering armhole with a V-shape at its base.

OPTIONAL REMOVABLE SHOULDER PADS

Size 6mm/US 10 needles
Velcro
Note 2 strands of yarn are used throughout.

Cast on 3 sts. **Row 1** (RS) K into front and back of st (inc 1), k1, inc 1. **Row 2** Knit. **Row 3** Inc 1, k3, inc 1. **Row 4** Knit. Continue to inc at beginning and end of every RS row until have 21 sts.

Next row (WS) K9, slip 2 tog as if to knit, knit next stitch, pass 2 slipped sts over knit st (S2kp2), k9—19 sts. [K 3 rows. **Next (dec) row** K to center 3 sts, S2kp2, k to end] 3 times—13 sts. [K 1 row. Work dec row.] 4 times—5 sts. Bind off.

Sew hook side only of a piece of Velcro to the center top of shoulder pad so it will grip the knitted fabric inside the garment's shoulder.

Chart A

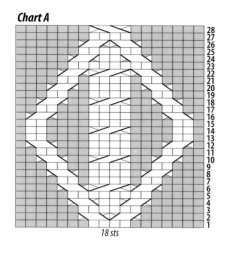

28 27 26 25 24 23 22 21 20 19 18 17 16 15 14 13 12 11 10 9 8 7 6 5 4 3 2 1

18 sts

Chart C

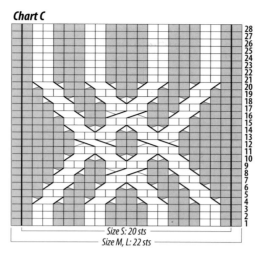

28 27 26 25 24 23 22 21 20 19 18 17 16 15 14 13 12 11 10 9 8 7 6 5 4 3 2 1

Size S: 20 sts
Size M, L: 22 sts

Chart D

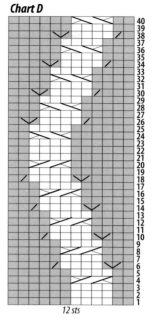

40 39 38 37 36 35 34 33 32 31 30 29 28 27 26 25 24 23 22 21 20 19 18 17 16 15 14 13 12 11 10 9 8 7 6 5 4 3 2 1

12 sts

Chart B

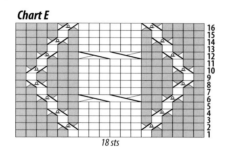

10 9 8 7 6 5 4 3 2 1

Size S: 8 sts
Size M, L: 10 sts

Chart E

16 15 14 13 12 11 10 9 8 7 6 5 4 3 2 1

18 sts

Patterns adapted for circular knitting from Barbara Walker's *Treasuries* 1 and 2.

how to

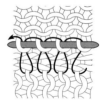

HALF-GRAFT AT UNDERARM

This is a perpendicular join (joining sts to rows). Bring yarn up from WS and weave under ladder between edge of steek and sleeve background sts. Then go across to first purl st, go through it and st next to it, then back across to next ladder by steek. Continue in this half-graft, easing on the side of the steek (by weaving under two ladders) if necessary.

Shoulder chart: Size S

3 steek sts

Shoulder chart: Size M

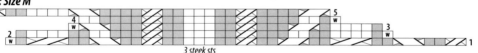

3 steek sts

Shoulder chart: Size L

3 steek sts

Body Pat Arrangement

0 (0, 5) sts Rev St st	0 (2, 2) sts 1/1 RT	8 (9, 9) sts Rev St st	2 sts 1/1 RT	18 sts Chart A	2 sts 1/1 RT	8 (10, 10) sts Chart B	2 sts 1/1 RT	20 (22, 22) sts Chart C	2 sts 1/1 RT	8 (10, 10) sts Chart B	2 sts 1/1 RT	18 sts Chart A	2 sts 1/1 RT	7 (9, 9) sts Rev St st	0 (0, 2) sts 1/1 RT	0 (0, 4) sts Rev St st

Sleeve Pat Arrangement

0 (3, 10) sts Rev St st	0 (2, 2) sts 1/1 RT	10 (9, 9) sts Rev St st	2 sts 1/1 RT	9 sts Rev St st	2 sts 1/1 RT	12 sts Chart D, beg rnd 21	2 sts 1/1 RT	18 sts Chart E	2 sts 1/1 RT	12 sts Chart D	2 sts 1/1 RT	9 sts Rev St st	2 sts 1/1 RT	10 (9, 9) sts Rev St st	0 (2, 2) sts 1/1 RT	0 (3, 10) sts Rev St st

The idea for a single sweater can come from many sources. Often, one garment is the result of taking a bit of trim from one place, a well-turned cable from another, and how about a rolled neck on this one? In the case of Celtic Geometry, the design came forth, fully realized, from the hands of a Celtic bronzesmith of the 7th century BC. The object he fashioned is a wide belt of stamped bronze, to be worn by a chieftain or warrior of very high rank. The central large motif and narrower side panels were all there, as well as the bottom border. All I had to do was translate bronze into wool! The pattern that follows is the result of these efforts.

Barbara Venishnick

Celtic geometry

Seed st *OVER ANY NUMBER OF STS*
Row 1 *K1, p1; rep from*. *Row 2* K the purl sts and p the knit sts. Rep Row 2 for Seed st.

Bobble pat *OVER A MULTIPLE OF 4 STS, PLUS 3*
Make Bobble (MB) K into front, back, front, back, front of st, turn, p5, turn, k5, turn, p2tog, p1, p2tog, turn, k3tog.
Rows 1, 3, 5, and 9 (RS) Knit. *Row 2* (WS) Knit. *Rows 4, 6, 8, and 10* Purl. *Row 7* *K3, MB; rep from*, end k3. *Rows 11 and 12* Purl.

Note
See *School*, p. 102, for 3-needle bind-off (ridge effect).

Back
Cast on 107 (111, 115) sts. Work 12 rows of Bobble pat. *Next row* (RS) Purl and inc 22 (24, 26) sts evenly across—129 (135, 141) sts. *Begin Chart pats and Seed st:*
Row 1 (WS) Work 9 (12, 15) sts in Seed st, place marker (pm), then reading charts from left to right, work 9 sts Chart A, pm, 13 sts Chart E, pm, 15 sts Chart C, pm, 37 sts Chart D, pm, 15 sts Chart C, pm, 13 sts Chart B, pm, 9 sts Chart A, pm, work 9 (12, 15) sts in Seed st. Continue in pats as established until piece measures 11½ (12, 12½)" from beginning, end with a WS row.

Skill Intermediate
Fit Loose
Sizes S (M, L). Shown in Medium.
Finished measurements 40 (42, 44)" around and 20¾ (21¾, 22¾)" long.
Gauge 20 sts and 32 rows to 10cm/4" over Seed st, using size 4mm/US 6 needles.
Yarn 2020 (2180, 2350) yds. Medium weight.
Needles Size 4mm/US 6, *or size to obtain gauge.*
Size 4mm/US 6 circular needle, 40cm/16" long.
Extras Cable needle (cn).
Stitch markers and holders.
Original yarn Cynthia Helene's Merino (superwash wool; 1¾oz/50g; 99 yds/90m).

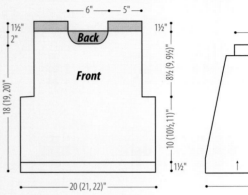

Shape armholes
Continue in pats, bind off 8 (11, 14) sts at beginning of next 2 rows—113 sts. Work even until armhole measures 8½ (9, 9½)", end with a WS row.
Shape shoulder tabs
Next row (RS) K35, place next 43 sts on hold, join 2nd ball of yarn, k35. *Next row* (WS) K and dec 4 sts evenly across each shoulder—31 sts each side. Work 12 rows of Bobble pat across each shoulder. Place all sts on hold.

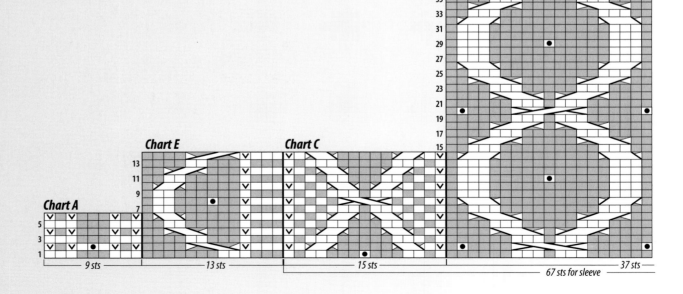

Front

Work as for Back until armhole measures 6½ (7, 7½)", end with a WS row.

Shape neck

Next row (RS) Work 39 sts in pat, place next 35 sts on hold, join 2nd ball of yarn, work 39 sts. Continue in pats, dec 1 st at each neck edge every other row 4 times—35 sts each side. Work even until armhole measures 8½ (9, 9½)", end with a WS row. **Next row** (RS) K and dec 4 sts evenly across each shoulder—31 sts each side. Place all sts on hold. With RS facing and WS tog, join shoulders, using 3-needle bind-off (ridge effect).

Sleeves

With RS facing, pick up and k113 (117, 121) sts along straight edge of armhole. **Begin Chart pats and Seed st: Row 1** (WS) Work 23 (25, 27) sts in Seed st, pm, 15 sts Chart C, pm, 37 sts Chart D, pm, 15 sts Chart C, pm, 23 (25, 27) sts in Seed st. Continue in pats as established, AT SAME TIME, when piece measures 2 (2½, 3)" from beginning, shape sleeves by dec 1 st each side every 6th row 19 times—75 (79, 83) sts. Work even until sleeve measures 17 (17½, 18)" from beginning, end with a WS row.

Shape cuff

K 2 rows, dec 13 (15, 17) sts evenly across each row—49 sts. Work 12 rows of Bobble pat, working Row 7 as follows: K2, *MB, k3; rep from*, end MB, k2. Bind off purlwise.

Finishing

Neckband

With RS facing and circular needle, k43 sts from back neck holder, dec 9 sts evenly spaced, pick up and k12 sts along left front neck, k35 sts from front holder, dec 13 sts evenly spaced, pick up and k12 sts along right front neck—80 sts. Pm, join and work in rnds as follows: P 1 rnd, k 1 rnd, p 1 rnd. K 4 rnds. **Next rnd** *K3, MB; rep from*. K 3 rnds. P 1 rnd, k 1 rnd, p 1 rnd, then k every rnd until piece measures 1¼" from last p rnd. Bind off loosely. Fold neckband at last p rnd and sew to WS. Sew side, sleeve, and underarm seams. ∩

☐ K on RS, p on WS

▦ P on RS, k on WS

☑ Slip 1 purlwise with yarn in back.

⦿ **MB (On RS)** K into front, back, front, back, front of st, turn, p5, turn, k5, turn, p2tog, p1, p2tog, turn, k3tog. **(On WS)** P into front, back, front, back, front of st, turn, k5, turn, p5, turn, k2tog, k1, k2tog, turn, p3tog.

2/1 RPC Sl 1 to cn, hold to back, k2; p1 from cn.

2/1 LPC Sl 2 to cn, hold to front, p1; k2 from cn.

2/2 RPC Sl 2 to cn, hold to back, k2; p2 from cn.

2/2 LPC Sl 2 to cn, hold to front, p2; k2 from cn.

2/3 RPC Sl 3 to cn, hold to back, k2; p3 from cn.

2/3 LPC Sl 2 to cn, hold to front, p3; k2 from cn.

3/1 RPC Sl 1 to cn, hold to back, k3; p1 from cn.

3/1 LPC Sl 3 to cn, hold to front, p1; k3 from cn.

3/2 RPC Sl 2 to cn, hold to back, k3; p2 from cn.

3/2 LPC Sl 3 to cn, hold to front, p2; k3 from cn.

2/1/2 LPC Sl 3 to cn, hold to front, k2; sl last p st from cn to LH needle and purl it; k2 from cn.

3/1/3 RPC Sl 4 to cn, hold to back, k3; sl last p st from cn to LH needle and purl it; k3 from cn.

3/1/3 LPC Sl 4 to cn, hold to front, k3; sl last p st from cn to LH needle and purl it; k3 from cn.

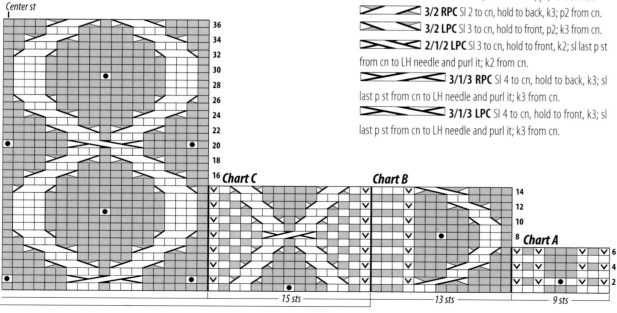

Center st

Chart C — 15 sts

Chart B — 13 sts

Chart A — 9 sts

Celtic geometry

future-forward Aran

One of the most versatile shapes in traditional Aran knitting is the diamond. To update this motif for a 'new millennium' look, the interior background of the diamond cable is worked in moss stitch to achieve a unique textural effect that complements the side panels of the garment. The diamond cables are then 'suspended' with simple rope cables and added onto the crisp lines of a twisted-stitch ladder. Mirrored open cables are interspersed between the diamond panels for added visual interest. Time-honored cables are presented in a new way.

Kathy Zimmerman

future-forward Aran

Note
See *School*, p. 102, for 3-needle bind-off.

Moss st *OVER AN ODD NUMBER OF STS*
Row 1 (RS) P1, *k1, p1; rep from*. *Rows 2 and 4* K the knit sts and p the purl sts. *Row 3* K1, *p1, k1; rep from*. Rep rows 1–4 for Moss st.

Back
With size 5mm (US 8) needles, cast on 128 (140, 152, 160, 172) sts. *Foundation row* (WS) P1, [k1, p1] 4 (7, 10, 12, 15) times, place marker (pm), *k4, p2, k2, p2, k4, pm, p2, k5, p4, k5, p2, pm, k4, p2, k2, p2, k4, pm*, p4, [k1, p1] 5 times, p4, pm, rep from * to * once, p1, [k1, p1] 4 (7, 10, 12, 15) times. *Begin Moss st and chart pats* (*Note* Begin all pats with row 1, except for center Chart B pat, which starts with chart row 23.) *Next row* (RS) Work 9 (15, 21, 25, 31) sts Moss st, 14 sts Chart A, 18 sts Chart B, 14 sts Chart A, work row 23 of Chart B over 18 sts, 14 sts Chart C, 18 sts Chart B, 14 sts Chart C, 9 (15, 21, 25, 31) sts Moss st. Continue in pats as established until piece measures approx 15¾ (16¼, 16½, 16¾, 17¼)" from beginning, end with row 36 (38, 40, 42, 2) of center Chart B pat.

Shape armholes
Bind off 10 (10, 10, 13, 15) sts at beginning of next 2 rows—108 (120, 132, 134, 142) sts. Work even until armhole measures approx 8¼ (8½, 8½, 9, 9)", end with row 2 (6, 8, 12, 16) of center Chart B pat.

Shape neck
Next row (RS) Continue pats, work 35 (40, 46, 46, 50) sts, join 2nd ball of yarn and bind off center 38 (40, 40, 42, 42) sts, work to end. Working both sides at same time, bind off from each neck edge 2 sts twice, 1 st once—30 (35, 41, 41, 45) sts each side. Work 1 row even. Armhole measures approx 9½ (9¾, 9¾, 10¼, 10¼)". Place sts on hold.

Front
Work as for back until armhole measures approx 6¾ (7, 7, 7, 7)", end with row 36 (40, 42, 44, 4) of center Chart B pat.

Shape neck
Next row (RS) Continue pats, work 38 (43, 49, 49, 53) sts, join 2nd ball of yarn and bind off center 32 (34, 34, 36, 36) sts, work to end. Working both sides at same time, bind off from each neck edge 2 sts twice, 1 st 4 times—30 (35, 41, 41, 45) sts each side. Work even until same length as back to shoulder. Place sts on hold.

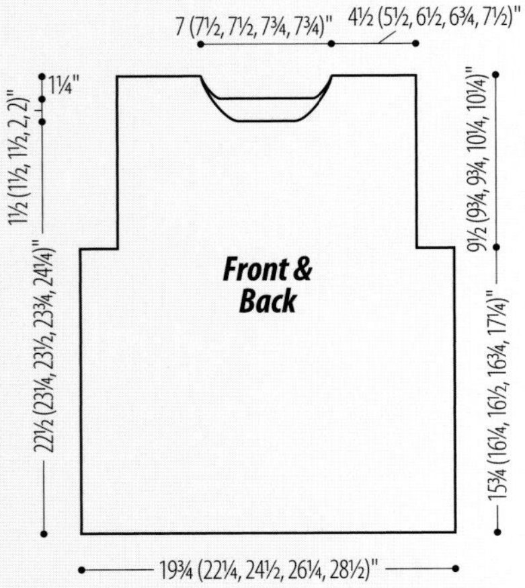

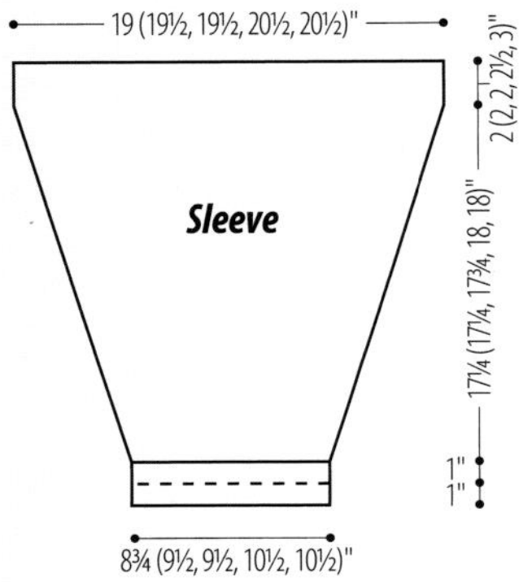

Sleeves
With size 4mm (US 6) needles, cast on 47 (49, 51, 53, 53) sts. [P 1 row, k 1 row]

twice, p 1 row. Change to size 3.5mm (US 4) needles. Work 2 rows k1, p1 rib. P 1 row (turning ridge). Work 2 rows k1, p1 rib. Change to size 4mm (US 6) needles. [P 1 row, k 1 row] 3 times, inc 9 (11, 9, 11, 11) sts evenly across last row—56 (60, 60, 64, 64) sts. Change to size 5mm (US 8) needles. *Foundation row* (WS) P1, [k1, p1] 2 (3, 3, 4, 4) times, pm, k4, p2, k2, p2, k4, pm, p2, k5, p4, k5, p2, pm, k4, p2, k2, p2, k4, p1, [k1, p1] 2 (3, 3, 4, 4) times. *Begin Moss st and chart pats: Row 1* (RS) Work 5 (7, 7, 9, 9) sts Moss st, 14 sts Chart A, 18 sts Chart B, 14 sts Chart C, 5 (7, 7, 9, 9) sts Moss st. Continue in pats as established, AT SAME TIME, inc 1 st each side (working incs into Moss st) on the next RS row, then every 4th row 21 (18, 16, 15, 15) times, every 6th row 4 (6, 8, 9, 9) times—108 (110, 110, 114, 114) sts. Piece measures approx 18¼ (18¼, 18¾, 19, 19)" above turning ridge. Work 2 (2, 2, 2½, 3)" even. Bind off.

Finishing
Block pieces. Join shoulders, using 3-needle bind-off.

Neckband
With RS facing and larger circular needle, begin at left shoulder and pick up and k13 (13, 13, 17, 17) sts along left front neck, 32 (34, 34, 36, 36) sts along center front neck, 13 (13, 13, 17, 17) sts along right front neck, 5 sts along right back neck, 38 (40, 40, 42, 42) sts along center back neck, 5 sts along left back neck—106 (110, 110, 122, 122) sts. Pm, join and work in rnds as follows: *Rnd 1* K13 (15, 15, 13, 13), [k2tog, k2] 8 (8, 8, 11, 11) times, k15 (16, 16, 15, 15), [k2tog, k4] 7 (7, 7, 8, 8) times, k2tog, k2 (3, 3, 0, 0)—90 (94, 94, 102, 102) sts. K 5 rnds. Change to smaller circular needle. Work 2 rnds k1, p1 rib. P 1 rnd (turning ridge). Work 2 rnds k1, p1 rib. Change to larger circular needle. K 6 rnds. Fold neckband to WS at turning ridge and sew open sts along pick-up rnd. Set in sleeves. Sew side and sleeve seams. ∩

Skill Intermediate
Fit Loose
Sizes S (M, L, 1X, 2X).
Shown in Medium.
Finished measurements 39½ (44½, 49, 52½, 57)" around and 25¼ (26, 26¼, 27, 27½)" long.
Gauge 20 sts and 26 rows equal 10cm/4" over Moss st, using size 5mm/US 8 needles.
Yarn 1875 (2110, 2275, 2510, 2700) yds.
Medium weight.
Needles Sizes 3.5, 4 and 5mm/US 4, 6 and 8, *or size to obtain gauge*.
Sizes 3.5 and 4mm/US 4 and 6 circular needle, 40cm/16" long.
Extras Cable needle (cn).
Stitch markers and holders.
Original yarn Skacel/Mondial's Eskimo (100% wool; 1¾ oz/50g; 88yds/80m).

Front & Back

Sleeve

7 (7½, 7½, 7¾, 7¾)" 4½ (5½, 6½, 6¾, 7½)"
11¼"
1½ (1½, 1½, 2, 2)"
9½ (9¾, 9¾, 10¼, 10¼)"
15¾ (16¼, 16½, 16¾, 17¼)"
22½ (23¾, 23½, 23¾, 24¼)"
19¾ (22¼, 24½, 26¼, 28½)"
19 (19½, 19½, 20½, 20½)"
2 (2, 2, 2½, 3)"
17¼ (17¼, 17¾, 18, 18)"
1"
1"
8¾ (9½, 9½, 10½, 10½)"

☐ K on RS, p on WS

▨ P on RS, k on WS

▨ **1/1 RT** K2tog, leaving sts on needle, then k first st again, sl both sts off needle.

▨ **1/1 LT** With RH needle behind work, k 2nd st on LH needle in back loop, k into front of first st, sl both sts off needle.

▨ **2/1 RC** Sl 1 to cn, hold to back, k2; k1 from cn.

▨ **2/1 RPC** Sl 1 to cn, hold to back, k2; p1 from cn.

▨ **2/1 LPC** Sl 2 to cn, hold to front, p1; k2 from cn.

▨ **2/2 RC** Sl 2 to cn, hold to back, k2; k2 from cn.

▨ **2/2 LC** Sl 2 to cn, hold to front, k2; k2 from cn.

▨ **2/2/2 RPC** Sl 4 to cn, hold to back, k2; sl 2 p sts from cn to LH needle, p2; k2 from cn.

▨ **2/2/2 LPC** Sl 4 to cn, hold to front, k2; sl 2 p sts from cn to LH needle, p2; k2 from cn.

Chart A

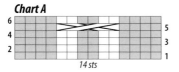

6   5
4   3
2   1

14 sts

Chart C

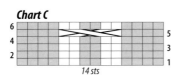

6   5
4   3
2   1

14 sts

Sleeve Pat Arrangement

5 (7, 7, 9, 9) sts Moss st	14 sts Chart C Beg row 1	18 sts Chart B Beg row 1	14 sts Chart A Beg row 1	5 (7, 7, 9, 9) sts Moss st

Body Pat Arrangement

9 (15, 21, 25, 31) sts Moss st	14 sts Chart C Beg row 1	18 sts Chart B Beg row 1	14 sts Chart C Beg row 1	18 sts Chart B Beg row 23	14 sts Chart A Beg row 1	18 sts Chart B Beg row 1	14 sts Chart A Beg row 1	9 (15, 21, 25, 31) sts Moss st

Chart B

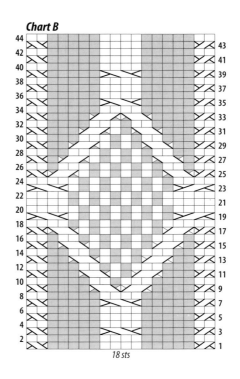

18 sts

Ever since I first saw those upside-down pictures of Arans in the backs of the now defunct **Mon Tricot** *stitch dictionaries some ten years ago, I have been intrigued with the idea of knitting these richly patterned sweaters from the neck down . . .*

Joan Schrouder

upside-down Aran

Notes
1 See *School*, p. 102, for ssk, loop cast-on, and invisible cast-on. **2** See Sizing Tips on p. 25. **3** Edge sts when working garter st are worked as follows (RS and WS): Slip first st purl-wise with yarn in front, k last st through back loop (tbl).

Neckband
With 16" needle and waste yarn, cast on 112 sts. Cut yarn. *Rnd 1* With working yarn, knit. *Rnd 2* Place marker (pm) and join, being careful not to twist sts, then *sl 1 with yarn in back (wyib), p1; rep from *. *Rnd 3* *K1 tbl, sl 1 with yarn in front (wyif); rep from *. *Rnd 4* *Sl 1 wyib, p1 tbl; rep from*. *Rnd 5* *K1, sl 1 wyif; rep from*. Remove waste yarn from beginning edge. *Rnd 6* *K1 tbl, p1; rep from *. *Rnd 7* *K1, p1 tbl; rep from *. Rep rnds 6 and 7 until piece measures approx 1¼". Leave sts on needle, using it as a holder.

Right saddle shoulder
With size 4mm/US 6 needle, work as follows: *Row 1* (RS) Work Chart A over 19 sts. Leaving rem sts on hold, work pat in rows as established until 53 (73) rows have been worked. Piece measures approx 5½ (7½)" from neckband. Place sts on hold. Do not cut yarn. Slip next 41 sts from neckband onto spare circular needle for holder for Front neck.

Left saddle shoulder
With a 2nd ball of yarn, work as for right shoulder over next 19 sts.

Back
With same ball of yarn, and RS facing, pick up and purl 26 (36) sts along back edge of left shoulder (both sides of the slip-st edge will be showing on the RS of garment), then work across rem 33 sts from neckband needle in established pat of neckband, then pick up and purl 26 (36) sts along back edge of right shoulder—85 (105) sts. *Next row* (WS) K0 (10), *k1, [loop cast-on 1 st, k2] 12 times, loop cast-on 1, k1*, k16, k in front and back of st, k16, work from * to *; k0 (10)—112 (132) sts. *Begin Charts: Row 1* (RS) Sl 1 wyif (edge st), work 4 (14) sts garter st, work Chart B over 30 sts, work Chart C beginning with row 21 over 42 sts, work Chart B over 30 sts, work 4 (14) sts garter st, k1 tbl (edge st). Continue in pat as established until 80 chart rows have been worked—piece from center of shoulder measures approx 10".

Shape armholes
At end of next 2 rows, using invisible cast-on, cast on 10 sts—132 (152) sts. Work 2 rows even working an edge st and 14 (24) sts garter st next to them. *Next (dec) row* (RS) Work edge st, k12 (22), k2tog, work to last 15 (25) sts, k2tog, work to end—130 (150) sts. Rep dec row every 10th row 9 times more working k2tog

in last 2 sts before Chart B row 5 is worked first time and in first 2 sts after Chart B row 5 is worked the 2nd time—112 (132) sts. Work 5 rows even, ending with row 40 of Chart C—piece measures approx 11" from armhole cast-on. Cut yarn. Place sts on hold.

Front
Right Front
With RS facing, beginning at front edge of right shoulder with attached yarn, pick up and p 26 (36) along front edge of right shoulder. *Next (inc) row* (WS) K1 (11), [loop cast-on 1, k2] 12 times, loop cast-on 1, k1—39 (49) sts. *Begin Charts: Row 1* (RS) Work edge st, work 4 (14) sts garter st, work Chart B over 30 sts, work row 1 of Chart D as follows: p3, ssk (1 st from shoulder and 1 st from neckband holder). Continue working patterns as established until Chart D is complete using 1 more st from neckband holder at end of each RS row—45 (55) sts. Do not cut yarn. Place sts on hold.

Left Front
With RS facing and 2nd ball of yarn, beginning where neckband sts on hold meet left shoulder, pick up and p 26 (36) sts along front edge of left shoulder. Work Inc

Skill Advanced
Fit Standard
Sizes S/M (L/1X). Shown in S/M.
Finished measurements 40 (48)" around and 24" long.
Gauge 20 sts equal 10cm/4" over Garter St (k every row), using size 4mm/US 6 needles.
Yarn 1400 (1800) yds. Medium weight.
Needles 4mm/US 6 circular, 24" (60cm) long, *or size to obtain gauge*. 3.5mm/US 4 circular, 40cm and 60cm/16" and 24" long. Four 3.5mm/US 4 double pointed (dpn).
Extras Stitch holders and markers. Cable needle (cn).
Original Yarn Henry's Attic Alpine Cotton (100% cotton, 800 yds/lb).

Back

6" — 5½ (7½)"

Left
Sleeve

20"

10"

16"

2½"

Front

11"

↑ *Direction of knitting*

3"

16 (20)"

20 (24)"

row as for Right Front—39 (49) sts. *Begin Charts: Row 1* (RS) Work Chart E over 4 sts, work Chart B over 30 sts, work 4 (14) sts garter st, work edge st. Continue working patterns as established until Chart E is complete using 1 st from neckband holder at end of every WS row—45 (55) sts. Cut yarn. *Next row* (RS) With RS facing, beginning at edge of Right Front with attached yarn, work edge st, work 4 (14) sts garter st, work Chart B over 30 sts, work first 20 sts of row 1 of Chart C (using neckband sts from holder when you come to them), k in front and back of next st, work last 20 sts of row 1 of Chart C, work Chart B over 30 sts, work 4 (14) sts garter st, work edge st—112 (132) sts. Continue in patterns as established until row 20 of Chart C has been completed the 2nd time (Front is same length as Back to armhole cast-on). Work as for Back beginning at shape armhole. Do not cut yarn. Do not place on hold.

Lower band

With RS facing and smaller 24" needle, work rnd 6 of neckband across Front and continue across Back, dec 40 (44) sts around, continuing pat into band where possible—184 (220) sts. Join and work rnd 7 of neckband. Rep these 2 rnds until rib measures 3". Bind off in pat.

Sew side seams as shown in illustration.

Sleeves

Left sleeve

Place 20 invisibly cast-on sts (10 from Front and 10 from Back) on a dpn for a holder, removing waste yarn. With WS facing and larger 24" needle, begin at dpn and pick up and knit (edge st will show on RS of garment) 41 sts along Back edge of armhole to shoulder, work in pat (row 4 of Chart A) across 19 shoulder sts, pick up and k 41 sts along front edge of armhole—101 sts. *Next row* (RS) K41, work 19 sts Chart A, k40, ssk (1 st from sleeve and 1 st from holder). *Next row* (WS) K41, work 19 sts Chart A, k40, p2tog (1 st from sleeve and 1 st from holder). Rep last 2 rows 9 times more (all sts from dpn used)—101 sts. Do not join, continue to work in rows, working first and last sts as edge sts. Work 2 rows even. *Next (dec) row* (RS) Work to 2 sts before Chart A, k2tog, work Chart A (row 7), k2tog, work to end. Rep dec row every 10th row 13 times more—73 sts. Work 1 row even.

Cuff

Change to dpns. *Row 1* (RS) K1, [k2tog] 13 times, work next 18 sts in pat, [k2tog] 14 times—46 sts. Pm, join and work in rnds as for rnds 6 and 7 of neckband. Sew sleeve seam as for side seam.

Right sleeve

Work as for left sleeve except begin to pick up and k sts along front of armhole to shoulder first. ∩

☐ K on RS, p on WS

■ P on RS, k on WS

☑ Slip st with yarn at WS

▣ K1 through back loop (tbl) on RS, p1 tbl on WS

◹ Ssk

◿ P2tog on WS

◺ P2tog on RS

▽ P into front and back of stitch

⧄ **1/1 RC (On WS)** Sl 1 to cn, hold to back, p1; p1 from cn.

⧅ **1/1 LC (On RS)** Sl 1 to cn, hold to front, k1; k1 from cn.
    (On WS) Sl 1 to cn, hold to front, p1; p1 from cn.

⧄ **1/1 RPC** Sl 1 to cn, hold to back, k1; p1 from cn.

⧅ **1/1 LPC** Sl 1 to cn, hold to front, p1; k1 from cn.

2/1 RPC Sl 1 to cn, hold to back, k2; p1 from cn.

2/1 LPC Sl 2 to cn, hold to front, p1; k2 from cn.

3/1 RPC Sl 1 to cn, hold to back, k3; p1 from cn.

3/1 LPC Sl 3 to cn, hold to front, p1; k3 from cn.

2/2 RC Sl 2 to cn, hold to back, k2; k2 from cn.

2/2 LC Sl 2 to cn, hold to front, k2; k2 from cn.

3/3 RC Sl 3 to cn, hold to back, k3; k3 from cn.

2/2/2 RPC Sl 4 to cn, hold to front, k2, sl 2 p sts from cn to LH needle, move cn to back, p2; k2 from cn.

3/4 R KTBL PC Sl 4 to cn, hold to back, k1 through back loop (tbl), p1, k1 tbl; [p1, k1 tbl] twice from cn.

3/4 L KTBL PC Sl 3 to cn, hold to front, [k1 through back loop (tbl), p1] twice; [k1 tbl, p1, k1 tbl] from cn.

Chart A

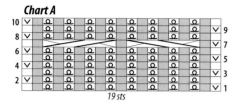

19 sts

Chart B

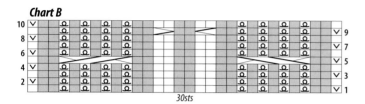

30 sts

Chart C

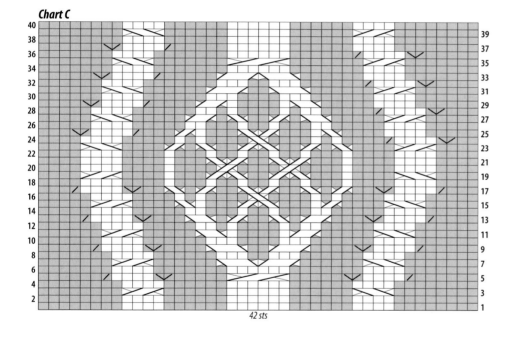

42 sts

Chart E   **Chart D**

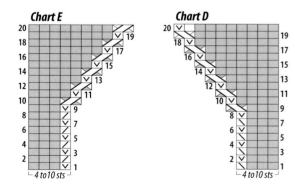

4 to 10 sts   4 to 10 sts

Back/Front Pat Arrangement

Edge st	4 (14) sts garter st	30 sts Chart B	42 sts Chart C Begin row 21	30 sts Chart B	4 (14) sts garter st	Edge st

knitter's tips:

sizing

The number of sts in the neckband is suitable for large children through medium adults. You can lengthen or shorten the width of the saddle shoulders and make compensatory adjustments in the number of garter sts in the Back and Front panels. You can lengthen or shorten the armhole length and make compensatory changes in the number of sts picked up for sleeves. You can increase or decrease the number of sts cast on for armholes and make compensatory changes in the number of sts in the garter st panels. You can lengthen or shorten the body from the armhole to the lower ribbing. Body can also be more or less tapered. However, whatever length changes you make, you should try to end the body on the last row of Chart C. You can shorten the ribbing to help with this adjustment. For shorter or longer sleeves, decrease more or less frequently and also take into account any changes you made in the length of the armhole because this will determine the width of the sleeve at underarm.

seaming

To make a decorative seam with the slipped edge, thread yarn through a blunt needle and sew seams as shown below. After seaming, a chain runs up both inside and outside garment.

*Visions of heavy cables and bobbles come to mind when I think of Aran sweaters. But not all Aran patterns are bulky. In her book, **Patterns for Guernseys, Jerseys & Arans**, Gladys Thompson includes numerous Aran patterns that are made primarily of twist stitches, little cables worked over two stitches. Since only single stitches cross, these fabrics are not as bulky as those made up of larger cables.*

Women of all sizes can wear a sweater constructed from twist-stitch Aran patterns and be flattered by the design. I have sized this sweater by varying three Aran patterns. The patterns are logical and easy to follow. After only a few rows, you will know the movement of the twist lines, so you won't have to refer to the graphs, and you'll find that the knitting is much faster.

Wendy Keele

Celtic pullover

Notes

1 See *School*, p. 102, for Make 1 purl (M1P). **2** Charts A–D are used for sizes XS, S and M and Charts E–H are used for sizes L, 1X and 2X.

Back

With smaller needles, cast on 106 (114, 126, 138, 146, 158) sts. *Row 1* (RS) *K1 through back loop (tbl), p1; rep from *. *Row 2* *K1, p1 tbl; rep from *. Rep these 2 rows until work measures 2 (2, 2½, 2½, 3, 3)", ending with row 1. Change to larger needles.

Note Work inc 1 as k in front and back of st.

For Sizes XS, S, M only: Next row (WS) [K2 (2, 12), inc 1, k1] 1 (2, 1) times, *p1 tbl, k2, p1 tbl, inc 1, p1 tbl, k2, p1 tbl*, [k1, inc 1] twice, k1, [p1 tbl] twice, inc 1, k5, work from * to * once, k1, inc 1, [k3, inc 1] twice, [p1 tbl, k1, p1 tbl, k2, p1 tbl, k1, p1 tbl] twice, k1, inc 1, [k3, inc 1] twice, **[p1 tbl, k2] twice, p1 tbl, inc 1, p1 tbl**, k2, inc 1, k3, [p1 tbl] twice, inc 1, k3, inc 1, work from ** to ** once, [k2, inc 1, k1] 1 (2, 0) times, [k2, inc 1, k11] 0 (0, 1) time—124 (134, 144) sts. *Begin Charts: Row 1* (RS) Work 5 (10, 15) sts Rev St st, *work Chart A over 10 sts, work Chart B over 16 sts, work Chart A over 10 sts*, work Chart C over 42 sts, work from * to * once, work 5 (10, 15) sts Rev St st.

For Sizes L, 1X, 2X only: Next row (WS) [K2 (2, 12), inc 1, k1] 1 (2, 1) times, * p1 tbl, k2, p1 tbl, k1, p1 tbl, inc 1, p1 tbl, k1, p1 tbl, k2, p1 tbl*, k3, inc 1, k2, p1 tbl, k1, [p1 tbl] twice, k1, p1 tbl, [k1, inc 1] twice, k1, work from * to * once, k1, inc 1, [k3, inc 1] twice, p1 tbl, k1, p1 tbl, inc 1, p1 tbl, k1, p1 tbl, k2, [p1 tbl, k1, p1 tbl] twice, [inc 1, p1 tbl, k1, p1 tbl] twice, k2, [inc 1, k3] twice, k1, **p1 tbl, inc 1, [p1 tbl, k1, p1 tbl, k2] twice, p1 tbl**, k2, inc 1, k1, inc 1, [p1 tbl, k1, p1 tbl] twice, k1, inc 1, k4, work from ** to ** once, [inc 1, k3] 1 (2, 0) times, [inc 1, k13] 0 (0, 1) time—158 (168, 178) sts. *Begin Charts: Row 1* (RS) Work 5 (10, 15) sts Rev St st, *work Chart E over 14 sts, work Chart F over 20 sts, work Chart E over 14 sts*, work Chart G over 52 sts, work from * to * once, work 5 (10, 15) sts Rev St st.

All sizes Continue in pats as established until Chart A (E) has been worked 9 (8) times.

Shape armholes

Bind off 1 (2, 2, 1, 2, 2) sts at beginning of next 8 rows—116 (118, 128, 150, 152, 162) sts. Work even until Chart C (G) has been completed 3 times from the beginning. Continue to work, replacing Chart C (G) with Chart D (H) and work until the 26 rows of D (H) have been completed. (*Note* There were 117 (119, 129, 149, 151, 161) sts after row 3 of D (H) was completed.) *Next row* (RS) Bind off 39 (39, 43, 51, 51, 55) sts for shoulder, cut yarn, place center 39 (41, 43, 47, 49, 51) sts on holder for back neck, join yarn and bind off rem 39 (39, 43, 51, 51, 55) sts for shoulder.

Front

Work as for Back through Row 14 of Chart D (H).

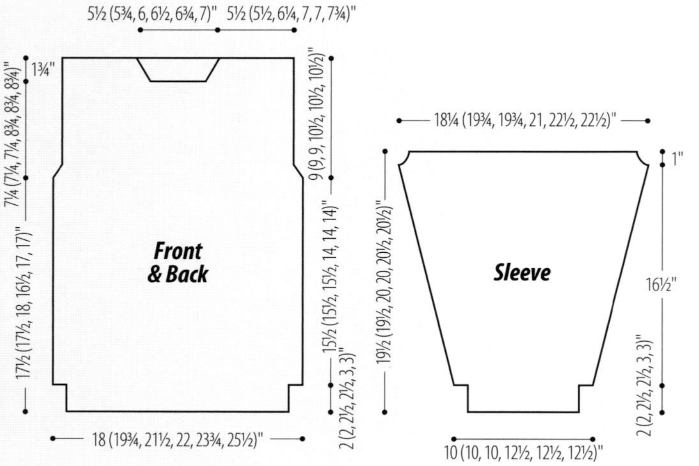

Shape neck

Next row (RS) Work 49 (49, 53, 66, 66, 70) sts, place next 19 (21, 23, 17, 19, 21) sts on hold, join 2nd ball of yarn and work to end. Working both sides at same time, work 1 row even. *Next row* (RS) Work to 2 (2, 2, 3, 3, 3) sts before neck edge, place these last 2 (2, 2, 3, 3, 3) sts on hold; 2nd side; neck edge, work 2 (2, 2, 3, 3, 3) sts (omitting a cross if it was omitted on first side) and place them on hold, work to end. Rep last 2 rows four times more—39 (39, 43, 51, 51, 55) sts each side. Work 1 row even. Bind off.

Sleeves

With smaller needles, cast on 44 (44, 44, 60, 60, 60) sts. Work rib as for back. Change to larger needles.

For sizes XS, S, M only: Next row (WS) K2, [inc 1, k1] 3 times, p1 tbl, k2, p1 tbl, [inc 1, p1 tbl] twice, k2, inc 1, k1, inc 1, [p1 tbl] twice, [k1, inc 1] twice, k1, p1 tbl, k2, p1 tbl, [inc 1, p1 tbl] twice, [inc 1, k1] 3 times, k2—58 sts. *Begin Charts: Row 1* (RS) work 11 sts Rev St st, work 10 sts Chart A, 16 sts Chart B, 10 sts chart A, work 11 sts Rev St st.

For sizes L, 1X, 2X only: Next row (WS) K2, [inc 1, k1] 4 times, k1, p1 tbl, inc 1 [p1 tbl, k1, p1 tbl, inc 1] twice, p1 tbl, [k1, inc 1] twice, k1, [p1 tbl, k1, p1 tbl] twice, [k1, inc 1] twice, k1, p1 tbl, k2, [p1 tbl, k1, p1 tbl, inc 1] twice, p1 tbl, [inc 1, k1] 5 times—78 sts. *Begin Charts: Row 1* (RS) Work 15 sts Rev St st, work 14 sts Chart E, 20 sts Chart F, 14 sts Chart E, work 15 sts Rev St st.

All Sizes Continue in pats as established, inc 1 st each side (working incs into Rev St st) on row 3 then every 4th row 22 (26, 26, 22, 26, 26) times more—104 (112, 112, 124, 132, 132) sts. Work even until 24 rows of Chart B (F) have been completed 4 times and rows 1–18 worked once more.

5½ (5¾, 6, 6½, 6¾, 7)"   5½ (5½, 6¼, 7, 7, 7¾)"

1¾"

7¼ (7¼, 7½, 8¾, 8¾, 8¾)"

9 (9, 9½, 10½, 10½, 10½)"

17½ (17½, 18, 16½, 17, 17)"

15½ (15½, 15½, 14, 14, 14)"

Front & Back

2 (2, 2½, 2½, 3, 3)"

18 (19¾, 21½, 22, 23¾, 25½)"

18¼ (19¾, 19¾, 21, 22½, 22½)"

1"

19½ (19½, 20, 20, 20½, 20½)"

16½"

Sleeve

2 (2, 2½, 2½, 3, 3)"

10 (10, 10, 12½, 12½, 12½)"

Skill Intermediate
Fit Loose
Sizes XS (S, M, L, 1X, 2X).
Shown in Large.
Finished measurements 36 (39½, 43, 44, 47½, 51)" around and 26½ (26½, 27, 27, 27½, 27½)" long.
Gauge 22 sts and 28 rows equals 10cm/4" over Rev St st (p on RS, k on WS) using larger needles.
Yarn 1765 (1910, 2060, 2180, 2375, 2490) yds. Medium weight yarn.
Needles 4.5 and 5mm/US 7 and 8, *or size to obtain gauge*; 4.5mm/US 7 circular 40cm/16" long.
Extras Cable needle (cn). Stitch holders.
Original yarn Lane Borgosesia Maratona (100% wool; 1¾ oz/50g, approx 121 yds/110m).

Chart E

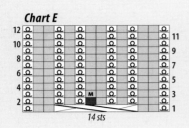

14 sts

Chart F

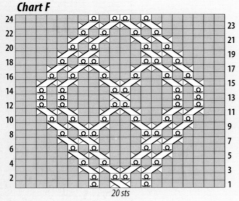

20 sts

Bind off 1 (2, 2, 1, 2, 2) sts at the beg of next 8 rows. Bind off remaining 96 (96, 96, 116, 116, 116) sts.

Finishing

Sew shoulders.

Neckband

With circular needle and RS facing, beginning with k1 tbl (p1, k1 tbl, k1 tbl, p1, k1 tbl), work in k1tbl, p1 rib across back neck sts from holder, pick up and p (k, p, p, k, p) one st at shoulder seam, continue in rib across 10 (10, 10, 15, 15, 15) sts on holders along left neck edge, 19 (21, 23, 17, 19, 21) sts from front holder,10 (10, 10, 15, 15, 15) sts on holders along right front neck edge, pick up and p (k, p, p, k, p) one st at right shoulder seam—80 (84, 88, 96, 100, 104) sts. Work even in rib for 2". Bind off loosely in rib.

Sew in sleeves. Sew side and sleeve seams. ∩

Chart G

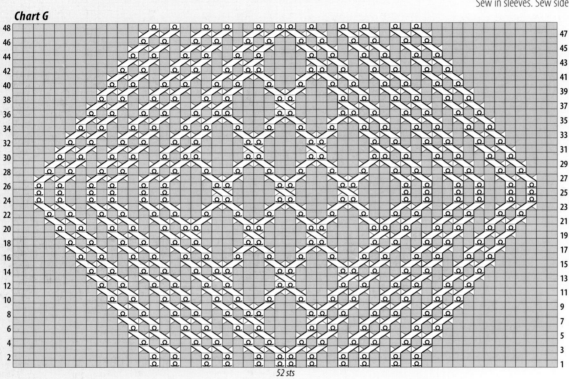

52 sts

▢ P on RS, k on WS

▣ K1 through back loop (tbl) on RS, p1 tbl on WS

■ No stitches exist in these areas of chart

M M1P Make 1 purl

◿ **P2tog**

◿◿ **1/1 RC tbl** Sl 1 to cn, hold to back, k1 tbl; k1 tbl from cn.

◺◺ **1/1 LC tbl** Sl 1 to cn, hold to front, k1 tbl; k1 tbl from cn.

◿◿ **1/1 RPC tbl** Sl 1 to cn, hold to back, k1 tbl; p1 from cn.

◺◺ **1/1 LPC tbl** Sl 1 to cn, hold to front, p1; k1 tbl from cn.

◺◺◺ **1/2 LC dec tbl** Sl 1 to cn, hold to front; pass 2nd st on LH needle over first st and off needle, k1tbl, p1; k1tbl from cn.

◺◺◺◺ **3/4 LC dec tbl**

Sl 3 to cn, hold to front; pass 2nd st on LH needle over first st and off needle, [k1tbl, p1] twice; k1tbl, p1, k1tbl from cn.

Chart H

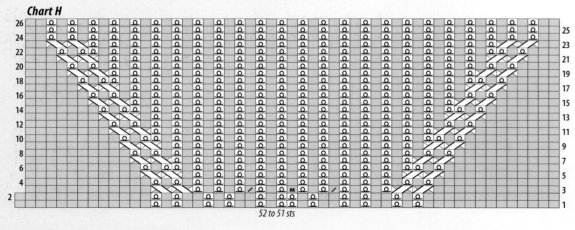

52 to 51 sts

Back/Front Pat Arrangement for L, 1X, 2X

5 (10, 15) sts Rev St st	14 sts Chart E	20 sts Chart F	14 sts Chart E	52 sts Chart G	14 sts Chart E	20 sts Chart F	14 sts Chart E	5 (10, 15) sts Rev St st

Sleeve Pat Arrangement for L, 1X, 2X

15 sts Rev St st	14 sts Chart E	20 sts Chart F	14 sts Chart E	15 sts Rev St st

Chart A

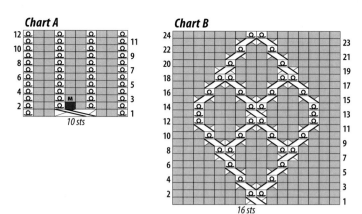

10 sts

Chart B

16 sts

Chart C

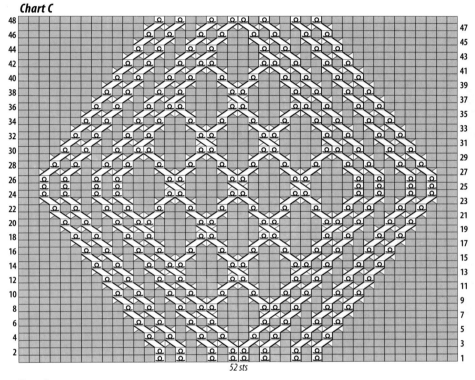

52 sts

Chart D

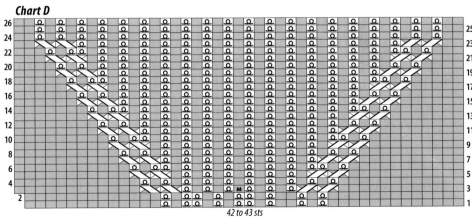

42 to 43 sts

Back/Front Pat Arrangement for XS, S, M

5 (10, 15) sts Rev St st	10 sts Chart A	16 sts Chart B	10 sts Chart A	42 sts Chart C	10 sts Chart A	16 sts Chart B	10 sts Chart A	5 (10, 15) sts Rev St st

Sleeve Pat Arrangement for XS, S, M

11 sts Rev St st	10 sts Chart A	16 sts Chart B	10 sts Chart A	11 sts Rev St st

unexpected Celtics

I am always amazed by the timeless beauty and the endless design possibilities of the Viking patterns. Here I wanted to do something thoroughly modern. The boat neck is very much in fashion, and so are the flared sleeves, though they also touch back on medieval fashion. The fitted shape and the vertical lines are feminine and flattering to the figure.

Elsebeth Lavold

Viking Turid

Notes

1 See *School*, p. 102, for ssk, lifted inc, and long-tail cast-on. **2** Use long-tail cast-on throughout. **3** Use lifted inc throughout, either right-slanting knit (RKI) or purl (RPI); or left-slanting knit (LKI), or purl (LPI), as indicated.

Back

With smaller needles, cast on 110 (118, 126, 134) sts. K 1 row. P 2 rows. Change to larger needles. *Next row* (RS) K31 (35, 39, 43), [p2, k21] twice, p2, k31 (35, 39, 43). K the knit sts and p the purl sts for 7 more rows. *Dec row* (RS) K1, k2tog, k to next purl rib, p2, k2tog, k to next purl rib, p2, k to 2 sts before next purl rib, ssk, p2, k to last 3 sts, ssk, k1—106 (114, 122, 130) sts. Rep dec row every 14th row 3 times more—94 (102, 110, 118) sts. Work 9 rows even. *Begin Chart pat: Row 1* (RS) K25 (29, 33, 37), place marker (pm), work chart pat over 44 sts, pm, k to end. Work 3 rows even, working chart pat between markers, and rem sts in St st. *Next row* (RS) K1, k2tog, work in pat to last 3 sts, ssk, k1—90 (98, 106, 114) sts. Work even through chart row 30. *Inc row 1* K1, RKI, work in pat to last 2 sts, LKI, k1—104 (112, 120, 128) sts. Rep inc row 1 every 10th row 3 times more—98 (106, 114, 122) sts. Work even through chart row 70 (remove markers after last row). *Inc row 2* K1, RKI, k to first purl rib, p2, RKI, k to next purl rib, p2, k to 1 st before next purl rib, LKI, p2, k to last 2 sts, LKI, k1—102 (110, 118, 126) sts. Work 9 rows even. Work inc row 2 once more—106 (114, 122, 130) sts. Continue to work incs at purl ribs ONLY every 10th row 2 (2, 3, 3) times more, AT SAME TIME, when 16 rows have been worked above chart and piece measures approx 18½" from beginning, shape armholes as follows:

Shape armholes

Bind off 6 sts at beginning of next 2 rows, 4 sts at beginning of next 2 (2, 4, 4) rows. *Next row* (RS) K1, k2tog, work to last 3 sts, ssk, k1. Rep last row every other row 2 (5, 4, 6) times more. Work even until armhole measures 7¾ (8¼, 9, 9½)", end with a WS row—84 (86, 90, 94) sts.

Shape shoulders and neck

Row 1 (RS) Bind off 9 (10, 10, 11) sts, k until there are 9 (9, 10, 11) sts on RH needle, pm, k48 (48, 50, 50), pm, k to end. *Row 2* Bind off 9 (10, 10, 11) sts, p to marker, k sts between markers, p to end. *Row 3* Bind off 9 (9, 10, 11) sts, p to next marker, k to end. *Row 4* Bind off 9 (9, 10, 11) sts, then bind off rem 48 (48, 50, 50) sts knitwise.

Front

Work as for back.

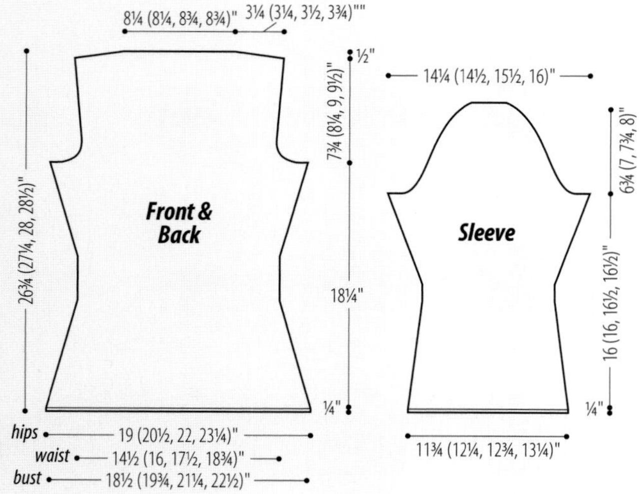

Sleeves

With smaller needles, cast on 68 (70, 74, 76) sts. K 1 row. P 2 rows. Change to larger needles. *Next row* (RS) K14 (15, 17, 18), [p2, k17] twice, p2, k14 (15, 17, 18). K the knit sts and p the purl sts for 3 more rows. *Begin Chart pat: Row 1* (RS) K12 (13, 15, 16), pm, work chart pat over 44 sts, pm, k to end. Continue working chart between markers, and rem sts in St st, through chart row 4. *Dec row* (RS) K1, k2tog, work in pat to last 3 sts, ssk, k1. Rep dec row every 14th row 4 times more —56 (58, 62, 64) sts. Work even through chart row 70. *Inc row* (RS) K1, RKI, [k to next purl rib, p2] 3 times, k to last 2 sts, LKI, k1. Rep inc row every 4th row 12 (12, 13, 13) times more—82 (84, 90, 92) sts. Work 5 rows even. Piece measures approx 16¼ (16¼, 16¾, 16¾)" from beginning.

Shape cap

Bind off 6 sts at beginning of next 2 rows. *Dec row* (RS) K1, k2tog, work to last 3 sts, ssk, k1. Rep dec row every 4th row 3 times more, then every other row 15 (16, 19, 20) times. Work 1 row even. Bind off 2 sts at beginning of next 8 rows. Bind off rem 16 sts.

Finishing

Block pieces. Sew shoulders and sides of neck. Set in sleeves. Sew side and sleeve seams. ⌒

Skill Intermediate
Fit Standard
Sizes S (M, L, 1X).
Shown in Small.
Gauge 23 sts and 32 rows equal 10cm/ 4" over St st, using larger needles.
Finished measurements 37 (39½, 42½, 45)" around, at bust, and 26¾ (27¼, 28, 28½)" long.
Yarn 1375 (1475, 1625, 1725) yds. Light weight.
Needles Size 3 and 3.5mm/US 2 and 4, *or size to obtain gauge.*
Extras Cable needle (cn). Stitch holders and markers.
Original yarn Rowan Wool Cotton (50% wool, 50 cotton; 1¾ oz/50g; 125 yds/113m).

Front & Back — 8¼ (8¼, 8¾, 8¾)" — 3¼ (3¼, 3½, 3¾)" — ½" — 7¾ (8¼, 9, 9½)" — 18¼" — 26¾ (27¼, 28, 28½)" — ¼"
hips — 19 (20½, 22, 23¼)"
waist — 14½ (16, 17½, 18¾)"
bust — 18½ (19¾, 21¼, 22½)"

Sleeve — 14¼ (14½, 15½, 16)" — 6¾ (7, 7¾, 8)" — 16 (16, 16½, 16½)" — ¼" — 11¾ (12¼, 12¾, 13¼)"

I used a symbol of luck, known as a St. John's cross, as the focal pattern. The symbol is incorporated into the design the same way it appears on the displayed buckle from Norway—placed in a diamond-shaped box. These types of buckles are often parodied, but no, they did not cover the nipples; they were worn higher up, fastening the shoulder straps of the dress.

☐ K on RS, p on WS

▨ P on RS, k on WS

▶ **RKI** Right knit inc

◀ **LKI** Left knit inc

▶ **RPI** Right purl inc

◀ **LPI** Left purl inc

K2tog on RS

Ssk on RS

K2tog on WS

Ssk on WS

■ No stitches exist in these areas of chart.

2/2 RC Sl 2 to cn, hold to back, k2; k2 from cn.

2/2 LC Sl 2 to cn, hold to front, k2; k2 from cn.

2/2 RPC Sl 2 to cn, hold to back, k2; p2 from cn.

2/2 LPC Sl 2 to cn, hold to front, p2; k2 from cn.

44 sts to 54 sts to 42 sts

Viking Turid

ornamental Celtic

Sometimes it is nice to approach things from a different angle, going against the grain, so to speak. I started this sweater from the 'sidelines.'

Elise Duvekot

ornamental Celtic

Notes

1 See *School*, p. 102, for ssk and Make 1 (M1). **2** Sweater back and front are knit from side to side. Sleeves are picked up and worked from top down.

Back

With larger needles, cast on 146 (154, 163) sts. P 1 row. ***Begin Charts: Row 1*** (RS) K2, place marker (pm), work 27 sts Chart A, pm, 16 (20, 20) sts Chart B, pm, 23 (23, 28) sts Chart C, pm, 14 sts Chart D, pm, 22 sts Chart E, pm, 15 (19, 23) sts Chart F, pm, 25 sts Chart G, pm, k2. Continue in pats as established until piece measures 21 (23, 25)" from beginning. Bind off.

Front

Work as for back until piece measures 7 (8, 9)" from beginning, end with a RS row. *Shape neck*

Next row (WS) Bind off 12 sts, work to end. ***Dec row*** (RS) Work to last 17 sts, k2tog (last 2 sts of Chart F), work to end. Rep Dec row every other row 11 times more—122 (130, 139) sts. Work even until piece measures 10½ (11½, 12½)" from beginning, end with a WS row. ***Inc row*** (RS) Work to last 15 sts, M1, work to end. Rep Inc row (working incs into Chart F) every other row 11 times more. Cast on 12 sts at beginning of next (WS) row, work to end (working added sts into Chart G and St st)—146 (154, 163) sts. Work even until piece measures 21 (23, 25)" from beginning. Bind off. Sew shoulders.

Sleeves

Place markers 10 (10½, 11)" down from shoulders on front and back for armholes. With RS facing and larger needles, pick up and k112 (116, 120) sts evenly between markers. K 3 rows. ***Begin Sleeve Chart: Row 1*** (RS) Begin as indicated for your size, work 28-st rep 4 times, end as indicated. Continue in chart pat as established, AT SAME TIME, dec 1 st each side every 4th row 5 times, every 6th row 14 (16, 18) times—74 sts. Work even until sleeve measures 15 (16, 17)" from beginning, end with a WS row. K 1 row. P 1 row, dec 1 st—73 sts. Change to smaller needles. *Work ribbing*

Row 1 (RS) P1, *k2, p1; rep from *. ***Row 2*** (WS) K1, *1/1 RT, k1; rep from *. Rep Rows 1 and 2 until ribbing measures 1½", end with a WS row. ***Next row*** (RS) P1, *k2tog, p1; rep from *. Bind off.

Finishing

Lower edge ribbing

With RS facing, and smaller needles, pick up and k175 (190, 205) sts evenly along lower edge of back. Work ribbing as for sleeve. Repeat for front. Sew side and sleeve seams, leaving ribbing at lower edges of front and back open. ∩

Skill Intermediate
Fit Loose
Sizes S (M, L). Shown in Small.
Finished measurements 42 (46, 50)" around and 22½ (24, 25½)" long.
Gauge 24 sts and 30 rows equal 10cm/4" in St st using larger needles.
Yarn 1920 (2200, 2490) yds. Light weight.
Needles Sizes 3.25mm and 4mm/US 3 and 6, *or size to obtain gauge*.
Extras Cable needle (cn). Stitch holders and markers.
Original yarn Anny Blatt/Grignasco Merino Gold (100% wool; 1¾oz/50g; 137 yds/125m).

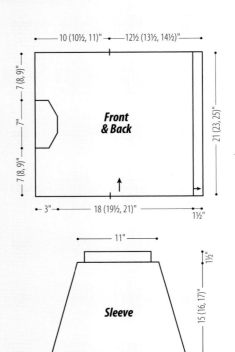

Front & Back — 10 (10½, 11)" · 12½ (13½, 14½)" · 21 (23, 25)" · 7 (8, 9)" · 7" · 7 (8, 9)" · 3" · 18 (19½, 21)" · 1½"

Sleeve — 11" · 1½" · 15 (16, 17)" · 20 (21, 22)"

□ K on RS, p on WS

▨ P on RS, k on WS

◸ Ssk on RS

◹ Ssk on WS

☑ K 1 through back loop (tbl) on RS, p 1 tbl on WS

Ⓜ **OPEN INC (on RS)** Insert LH needle from back to front under strand between st just worked and next st on LH needle, k this strand through back loop, creating an open st.

Ⓜ **OPEN INC (on WS)** Same as Open Inc on RS

☉ Yarn over

■ No stitch exists in this area of chart.

☐ **YO LC** Yo, k2, pass yo over k2.

⧄⧅ **1/1 RT (on RS)** K2tog and leave sts on LH needle, insert RH needle between 2 sts just knit, and k the first st; sl both sts off needle.

(on WS) Skip first st and p 2nd st, then p skipped st; sl both sts from needle.

⧅⧄ **1/1 LT** With RH needle behind work, k 2nd st on LH needle through back loop, then k skipped st through front loop; sl both sts off needle.

⧄⧅ **1/2 LC DEC** K3, pass 3rd st on RH needle over first 2 sts.

⧄ **3/2 RPC** Sl 2 to cn, hold to back, k3; p2 from cn.

⧅ **3/2 LPC** Sl 3 to cn, hold to front, p2; k3 from cn.

⧄ **3/3 RC** Sl 3 to cn, hold to back, k3; k3 from cn.

⧅ **3/3 LC** Sl 3 to cn, hold to front, k3; k3 from cn.

Sleeve Chart

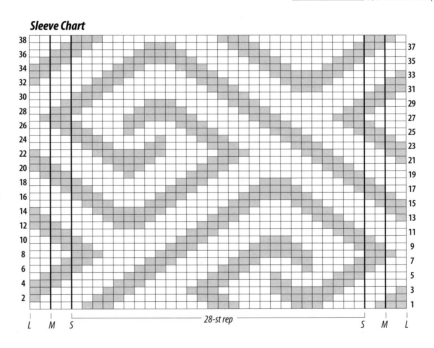

L M S ⟵ 28-st rep ⟶ S M L

Chart A

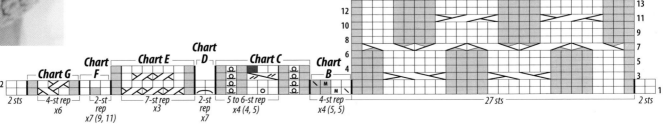

Chart G
2 sts

Chart G
4-st rep x6

Chart F
2-st rep x7 (9, 11)

Chart E
7-st rep x3

Chart D
2-st rep x7

Chart C
5 to 6-st rep x4 (4, 5)

Chart B
4-st rep x4 (5, 5)

27 sts

2 sts

*My knotted idea evolved from library research that led me to **The Book of Kells** and Celtic legends. I also found Alice Starmore's **The Celtic Collection** an inspiration.*

Melissa Leapman

symbolic knots

Seed St

Row 1 (RS) *K1, p1; rep from*. *Row 2* K the purl sts and p the knit sts. Rep Row 2 for Seed st.

Back

Cast on 81 (89, 97) sts. Work in Seed st until piece measures 15" from beginning, end with a WS row.

Shape armholes

Bind off 5 sts at beginning of next 2 rows—71 (79, 87) sts. Work even until armhole measures 8 (8½, 9)", end with a WS row.

Shape neck

Next row (RS) Work 22 (25, 28) sts, join 2nd ball of yarn and bind off center 27 (29, 31) sts, work to end. Working both sides at same time, dec 1 st at each neck edge every RS row twice—20 (23, 26) sts each side. Bind off.

Front

Work as for back until piece measures 6½ (7, 7½)" from beginning, end with a WS row. *Begin Celtic Knot Chart: Row 1* (RS) Work 16 (20, 24) sts in Seed st, place marker (pm), work row 1 of Celtic Knot Chart over 49 sts, pm, work to end. Continue in pats as established, working chart between markers, and shaping armholes when piece measures same length as back to armhole. Work even until armhole measures 7 (7½, 8)", end with a WS row. *Note* After chart row 87 has been worked, continue in Seed st over all sts.

Shape neck

Next row (RS) Work 29 (32, 35) sts, join 2nd ball of yarn and bind off center 13 (15, 17) sts, work to end. Working both sides at same time, bind off from each neck edge 3 sts once, 2 sts twice. Dec 1 st at each neck edge every RS row twice—20 (23, 26) sts each side. Work even until piece measures same length as back to shoulders. Bind off.

Sleeves

Cast on 39 (41, 43) sts. Work 1" in Seed st. Continue in Seed st, inc 1 st each side (working incs into pat) every 6th row 13 (15, 18) times, then every 8th row 4 (3, 1) times—73 (77, 81) sts. Work even until piece measures 18 (18½, 19)" from beginning. Bind off.

Finishing

Block pieces. Sew shoulders. Sew top of sleeves to straight edge of armholes, then sew sides of sleeve to bound-off armhole sts. Sew side and sleeve seams, leaving lower 4½" of body open on each side for side slits.

Skill Intermediate
Fit Loose
Sizes S (M, L). Shown in Medium.
Finished measurements 40 (44, 48)" around and 24 (24½, 25)" long.
Gauge 16 sts and 26 rows to 10cm/4" over Seed st using size 5mm/US 8.
Yarns 1190 (1320, 1455) yds. Medium weight.
Needles Size 5mm/US 8, *or size to obtain gauge*.
Size 5mm/US 8 circular needle, 40cm/16" long.
Extras Cable needle (cn).
Stitch markers and holders.
Original yarn Cascade Pastaza (50% llama, 50% wool; 3½oz/100g; 132yds/120m).

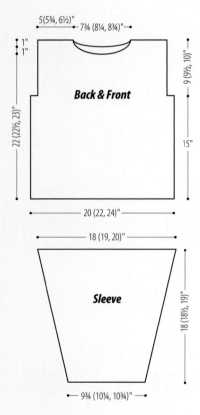

Neckband

With RS facing, and circular needle, pick up and k98 (104, 110) sts evenly around neck edge. Pm, join and work in k1, p1 rib for 4". Bind off loosely in rib. ∩

□ K on RS, p on WS

▨ P on RS, k on WS

▶ K into front and back of st

▼ K1, p1, k1 in a st

◪ P2tog on WS

■ No stitches exist in these areas of chart.

▲ **DEC 4** Sl 3 knitwise, one at a time, to RH needle; *pass 2nd st on RH needle over last st (center st) and off needle; sl center st back to LH needle; sl 2nd st on LH needle over center st and off needle;*sl center st back to RH needle; rep from * to * once; p1.

⟋⟍ **3/1 RPC** Sl 1 to cn, hold to back, k3; p1 from cn.

⟍⟋ **3/1 LPC** Sl 3 to cn, hold to front, p1; k3 from cn.

⟋⟍ **3/2 RPC** Sl 2 to cn, hold to back, k3; p2 from cn.

⟍⟋ **3/2 LPC** Sl 3 to cn, hold to front, p2; k3 from cn.

⟋⟍ **3/3 RC** Sl 3 to cn, hold to back, k3; k3 from cn.

⟍⟋ **3/3 LC** Sl 3 to cn, hold to front, k3; k3 from cn.

Celtic Knot Chart

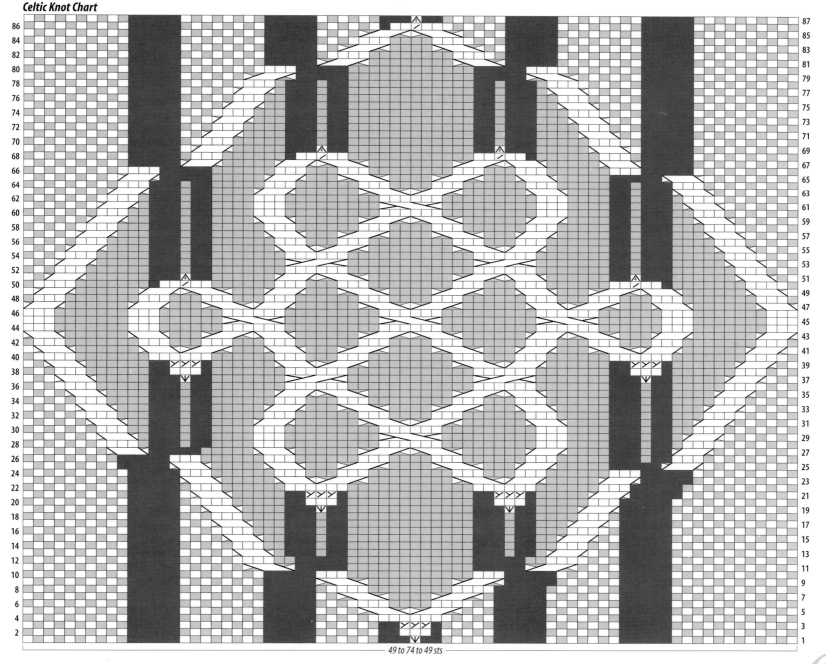

49 to 74 to 49 sts

symbolic knots

Swedish Thora

Elsebeth Lavold

Notes

1 See *School*, p. 102, for lifted inc, ssk, and ssp. **2** K first and last st of every row for selvage. **3** Use lifted inc throughout, either right-slanting knit (RKI) or purl (RPI), or left-slanting knit (LKI) or purl (LPI), as indicated.

Moss st *OVER ANY NUMBER OF STS*
Row 1 (RS) *K1, p1; rep from*. **Rows 2 and 4** K the knit sts and p the purl sts. **Row 3** *P1, k1; rep from*. Rep rows 1–4 for Moss st.

Skill Advanced
Fit Loose
Sizes S (M, L, 1X). Shown in Medium.
Finished measurements 39 (41¾, 47½, 50½)" around when buttoned, and 26 (27, 27, 28)" long, including ½ sleeve saddle.
Gauge 23 sts and 34 rows equal 10cm/4" over Moss st, using larger needles.
Yarn 1710 (1920, 2120, 2290) yds. Light weight.
Needles Size 3 and 3.5mm/US 3 and 4, *or size to obtain gauge.*
Buttons Seven 15mm/⅝".
Extras Cable needle (cn). Stitch markers and holders.
Original yarn Westminster Fibers/ Rowan's Designer DK (100% wool; 1¾oz/50g; 127yd/115m).

Swedish Thora

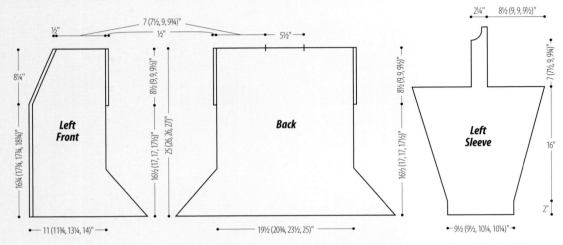

Back

With smaller needles, cast on 182 (190, 206, 214) sts. *Foundation row* (WS) P27 (29, 33, 35), k36, p25 (27, 31, 33), k6, p25 (27, 31, 33), k36, p27 (29, 33, 35). *Begin Charts A and B, and Moss st: Row 1* (RS) K1, p1, k2, p1, work 19 (21, 25, 27) sts in Moss st, p1, work 40 sts Chart A, p1, 19 (21, 25, 27) sts Moss st, p1, 10 sts Chart B, p1, 19 (21, 25, 27) sts Moss st, p1, 40 sts Chart A, p1, 19 (21, 25, 27) sts Moss st, p1, k2, p1, k1. *Row 2* K2, p2, k1, work 19 (21, 25, 27) sts Moss st, k1, 40 sts Chart A, k1, 19 (21, 25, 27) sts Moss st, k1, 10 sts Chart B, k1, 19 (21, 25, 27) sts Moss st, k1, 40 sts Chart A, k1, 19 (21, 25, 27) sts Moss st, k1, p2, k2. Work 2 rows even in pat. Change to larger needles. Continue in pats as established through row 20 of Chart B. Rep rows 13–20 of Chart B and continue all other pats as established, through row 66 of Chart A. Rep rows 65 and 66 of Chart A and continue all other pats as established, until 8-row rep of Chart B has been worked a total of 16 (16, 16, 17) times, then work chart rows 0 (13–16, 13–16, 0) once more. Piece measures approx 16½ (17, 17, 17½)" from beginning—120 (128, 144, 152) sts.
Shape armholes
Next row (RS) Cast on 3 sts and k3, p2, k2, p1, work in pat to end. *Next row* Cast on 3 sts and k1, p2, k2, p1, work in pat to last 8 sts, k1, p2, k2, p2, k1—126 (134, 150, 158) sts. Work even until armhole measures approx 7½ (8, 8, 8½)", end with row 20 of Chart B. Work rows 21–28 of Chart B—122 (130, 146, 154) sts. Armhole measures approx 8½ (9, 9, 9½)". Bind off.

Left Front

With smaller needles, cast on 98 (102, 110, 114) sts. *Foundation row* (WS) K1, p3, k6, p25 (27, 31, 33), k36, p27 (29, 33, 35). *Begin Charts A and B, and Moss st: Row 1* (RS) K1, p1, k2, p1, work 19 (21, 25, 27) sts in Moss st, p1, work 40 sts Chart A, p1,

19 (21, 25, 27) sts Moss st, p1, 10 sts Chart B, k2. *Row 2* K1, p1, work 10 sts Chart B, k1, 19 (21, 25, 27) sts Moss st, k1, 40 sts Chart A, k1, 19 (21, 25, 27) sts Moss st, k1, p2, k2. Continue in pats as for back until piece measures same length as back to armhole—70 (74, 82, 86) sts.
Shape armhole

Size S only: Next row (RS) Cast on 3 sts and k3, p2, k2, p1, work in pat to last 18 sts, work row 21 of Chart B over 16 sts, k2—73 sts. *Next row* K1, p1, work row 22 of Chart B over 16 sts, work in pat to last 8 sts, k1, p2, k2, p2, k1.
Sizes M, L, 1X only: Next row (RS) Cast on 3 sts and k3, p2, k2, p1, work in pat to end—77 (85, 89) sts. *Next row* Work in pat to last 8 sts, k1, p2, k2, p2, k1. Work through row 20 of Chart B, then work chart rows 21 and 22.
All sizes Armhole measures approx ¼ (¾, ¾, 1¼)".
Shape neck

Work through row 28 of Chart B, then work center sts of chart in rev St st, AT SAME TIME, dec at neck edge as follows: *Dec row 1* (RS) Work to last 6 sts, p2tog, k4. Rep Dec row 1 every other row 5 times more. Work 1 row even. *Dec row 2* (RS) Work to last 10 sts, p2tog, k2, p2, k4. Rep Dec row 2 every 4th row 13 times more—49 (53, 61, 65) sts. Work even until armhole measures same length as back to shoulder, end with a WS row. *Next row* (RS) Bind off 44 (48, 56, 60) sts, place rem 5 sts on hold. Using photo as guide, place 7 markers for buttons in cables along left front edge, with the first in center of top cable, and one each in center of every other cable below.

Right Front

(*Note* Work buttonholes on RS rows opposite markers as follows: Work 8 sts, bind off 3 sts, work to end. On following row, cast on 3 sts over bound-off sts.)

With smaller needles, cast on 98 (102, 110, 114) sts. **Foundation row** (WS) P27 (29, 33, 35), k36, p25 (27, 31, 33), k6, p3, k1. **Begin Charts A and B, and Moss st: Row 1** (RS) K2, work 10 sts Chart B, p1, work 19 (21, 25, 27) sts in Moss st, p1, 40 sts Chart A, p1, 19 (21, 25, 27) sts Moss st, p1, k2, p1, k1. **2** K2, p2, k1, work 19 (21, 25, 27) sts Moss st, k1, 40 sts Chart A, k1, 19 (21, 25, 27) sts Moss st, k1, 10 sts Chart B, p1, k1. Continue in pats as for back, working buttonholes opposite left front markers, until piece measures same length as back to armhole, end with a WS row—70 (74, 82, 86) sts.

Left Front Pat Arrangement

1 st garter st	1 st St st	10 sts Chart B	1 st Rev St st	19 (21, 25, 27) sts Moss St	1 st Rev St st	40 sts Chart A	1 st Rev St st	19 (21, 25, 27) sts Moss St	p1, k2, p1 rib	1 st garter st

Right Front Pat Arrangement

1 st garter st	p1, k2, p1 rib	19 (21, 25, 27) sts Moss St	1 st Rev St st	40 sts Chart A	1 st Rev St st	19 (21, 25, 27) sts Moss St	1 st Rev St st	10 sts Chart B	1 st St st	1 st garter st

Sleeve Pat Arrangement

p1, k2 rib	18 (18, 20, 20) sts Moss St	1 st Rev St st	10 sts Chart B	1 st Rev St st	18 (18, 20, 20) sts Moss St	k2, p1 rib

Legend:
- ☐ K on RS, p on WS
- ▨ P on RS, k on WS
- ⊠ **RKI** Right knit inc
- ⊠ **LKI** Left knit inc
- ▨ **RPI** Right purl inc
- ▨ **LPI** Left purl inc
- ▨ K2tog on RS
- ◩ Ssk on RS
- ▨ K2tog on WS
- ◩ Ssk on WS
- ■ No stitches exist in these areas of chart.
- **2/2 RC** Sl 2 to cn, hold to back, k2; k2 from cn.
- **2/2 LC** Sl 2 to cn, hold to front, k2; k2 from cn.
- **2/2 RPC** Sl 2 to cn, hold to back, k2; p2 from cn.
- **2/2 LPC** Sl 2 to cn, hold to front, p2; k2 from cn.

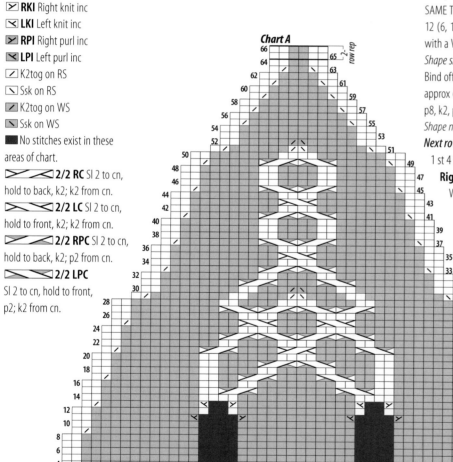

Chart A

40 to 6 sts

Shape armhole

Size S only: Next row (RS) K2, work row 21 of Chart B over 16 sts (working last buttonhole), work to end. **Next row** Cast on 3 sts and k1, p2, k2, p2, k1, work to last 18 sts, work row 22 of Chart B over 16 sts, p1, k1—73 sts.

Sizes M, L, 1X only Work 1 row even. **Next row** (WS) Cast on 3 sts and k1, p2, k2, p2, k1, work to end—77 (85, 89) sts. Work through row 20 of Chart B, then work chart rows 21 and 22. **All sizes** Armhole measures approx ¼ (¾, ¾, 1¼)".

Shape neck

Work to correspond to left front, reversing shaping. Work dec rows as follows: **Dec row 1** (RS) K4, ssp, work to end. **Dec row 2** (RS) K4, p2, k2, ssp, work to end.

Left Sleeve

With smaller needles, cast on 54 (54, 58, 58) sts. **Foundation row** (WS) P24 (24, 26, 26), k6, p24 (24, 26, 26). **Begin Charts A and B, and Moss st: Row 1** (RS) K2, p1, work 18 (18, 20, 20) sts Moss st, p1, 10 sts Chart B, p1, 18 (18, 20, 20) sts Moss st, p1, k2. **Row 2** K1, p1, k1, work 18 (18, 20, 20) sts Moss st, k1, 10 sts Chart B, k1, 18 (18, 20, 20) sts Moss st, k1, p1, k1. Work 2 rows even in pat. Change to larger needles. Continue in pats as established until sleeve measures 2" from beginning, end with a WS row. **Next (inc) row** (RS) K2, p1, work right lifted inc, work to last 4 sts, work left lifted inc, p1, k2. Continue in pats, AT SAME TIME, work inc row (working incs into Moss st) every 4th row 14 (23, 17, 26) times, every 6th row 12 (6, 10, 4) times—114 (120, 120, 126) sts. Work even until piece measures 18" from beginning, end with a WS row.

Shape sleeve saddle

Bind off 48 (51, 51, 54) sts at beginning of next 2 rows. Work even on rem 18 sts until saddle measures approx 6 (6½, 8, 8¾)", end with chart row 20. Work chart rows 21–28—14 sts. **Next row** (RS) P1, k2, p8, k2, p1.

Shape neck

Next row (WS) Bind off 6 sts (neck edge), work to end. Continue to bind off at neck edge every other row 1 st 4 times. Work 1 row even. Place rem 4 sts on hold.

Right Sleeve

Work as for left sleeve, reversing saddle neck shaping.

Finishing

Block pieces. Sew short side of saddle along each front shoulder. Work in pat across 5 sts of left front on hold until piece fits along curved edge of saddle, end with a RS row. **Next row** (WS) K1, p3, k1, then k1, p2, k1 across 4 saddle sts on hold—9 sts. Work until piece fits to center back neck. Bind off. Work right neck to correspond. Sew neckband to top of saddle along curved edge. Sew neckband at center back neck. Sew sides of saddle and neckband along top of back, centering neckband seam. Sew in sleeves. Sew side and sleeve seams. Sew on buttons. ∩

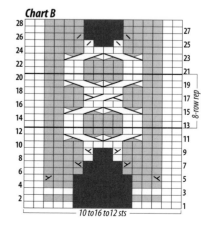

Chart B

10 to 16 to 12 sts

8-row rep

Back Pat Arrangement

1 st garter st	p1, k2, p1 rib	19 (21, 25, 27) sts Moss St	1 st Rev St st	40 sts Chart A	1 st Rev St st	19 (21, 25, 27) sts Moss St	1 st Rev St st	10 sts Chart B	1 st Rev St st	19 (21, 25, 27) sts Moss St	1 st Rev St st	40 sts Chart A	1 st Rev St st	19 (21, 25, 27) sts Moss St	p1, k2, p1 rib	1 st garter st

vests & jackets

Ann Regis

sensational shirttail

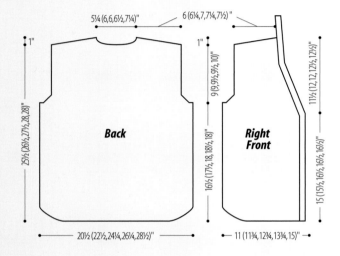

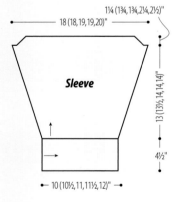

Notes

1 See *School*, p. 102, for Make 1 (M1), cable cast-on, and backwards single crochet.
2 Sl sts purlwise with yarn in back.

Moss st

Row 1 (RS) *K1, p1; rep from*. *Rows 2 and 4* K the knit sts and p the purl sts. *Row 3* *P1, k1; rep from*. Rep Rows 1—4 for Moss st.

Back

Cast on 48 (52, 56, 60, 66) sts. *Foundation row 1* (WS) P8 (9, 11, 12, 14), k2, p4, k2, p1, [p1, k1] 7 (8, 8, 9, 10) times, p1, k2, p4, k2, p8 (9, 11, 12, 14), cast on 2 sts, using cable cast-on. *Row 2* K10 (11, 13, 14, 16), *p2, k1, M1, k2, M1, k1, p2*, sl 1, work row 1 of Moss st over 14 (16, 16, 18, 20) sts, sl 1, rep from * to * once, k8 (9, 11, 12, 14), cast on 2 sts. *Row 3* P10 (11, 13, 14, 16), k2, p6, k2, p1, work row 2 of Moss st over 14 (16, 16, 18, 20) sts, p1, k2, p6, k2, p10 (11, 13, 14, 16), cast on 2 sts. *Begin Charts A and B: Row 1* (RS) K12 (13, 15, 16, 18), work 10 sts Chart A, sl 1, work Moss st as established over 14 (16, 16, 18, 20) sts, sl 1, work 10 sts Chart B, k10 (11, 13, 14, 16), cast on 2 sts. Continue in pats as established, casting on 2 sts at end of next 2 rows (working incs into St st), then inc 1 st each side every RS row 3 (4, 5, 6, 7) times—70 (76, 82, 88, 96) sts. Mark each side of last inc row. Work even until piece measures 16½ (17½, 18, 18½, 18)" from beginning, end with a WS row.

Shape armholes

Bind off 3 (3, 4, 4, 5) sts at beginning of next 2 rows. Dec 1 st each side every RS row 2 (3, 3, 4, 5) times—60 (64, 68, 72, 76) sts. Work even until armhole measures 4½", end with a WS row. *Next row* (RS) Work Moss st over 12 (13, 15, 16, 17) sts, work 36 (38, 38, 40, 42) sts in pats as established, work Moss st to end. Work even, working Moss st in place of St st, until armhole measures 9 (9, 9½, 9½, 10)", end with a WS row. Mark center 16 (18, 18, 20, 22) sts.

Shape shoulders and neck

Bind off 10 (11, 12, 12, 13) sts at beginning of next 2 rows, 11 (11, 12, 13, 13) sts at beginning of next 2 rows, AT SAME TIME, bind off marked sts and working both sides at same time, dec 1 st at each neck edge once.

Right Front

Cast on 27 (29, 31, 33, 36) sts. *Foundation row 1* (WS) P8 (9, 11, 12, 14), k2, p4, k2, p1, k0 (1, 1, 0, 1), [p1, k1] 5 (5, 5, 6, 6) times. *Row 2* [K1, sl 1] twice, work row 1 of Moss st over 6 (7, 7, 8, 9) sts, sl 1, p2, k1, M1, k2, M1, k1, p2, k8 (9, 11, 12, 14), cast on 2 sts. *Row 3* P10 (11, 13, 14, 16), k2, p6, k2, p1, work row 2 of Moss st

over 6 (7, 7, 8, 9) sts, [p1, k1] twice. *Begin Chart B: Row 1* (RS) [K1, sl 1] twice, work Moss st as established over 6 (7, 7, 8, 9) sts, sl 1, work 10 sts Chart B, k10 (11, 13, 14, 16), cast on 2 sts. Continue in pats as established, casting on 2 sts at end of next RS row, then inc 1 st at same edge every other row 3 (4, 5, 6, 7) times—38 (41, 44, 47, 51) sts. Mark end of last inc row. Work even until piece measures 15 (15½, 16½, 16½, 16½)" from beginning, end with a WS row.

Shape V-neck

Next (dec) row (RS) [K1, sl 1] twice, work 2 sts tog, work in pat to end. Rep dec row every 4th row 2 (4, 4, 6, 9) times more, then every 6th row 5 (4, 4, 3, 1) times, AT SAME TIME, when piece measures same as back to armhole, shape armhole as for back (and work Moss st in place of St st when armhole measures 4½")—25 (26, 28, 29, 30) sts. Work until armhole measures same as back to shoulder. Shape shoulder as for back. Work even on rem 4 sts until band fits along back neck to center back. Bind off.

Left Front

Cast on 27 (29, 31, 33, 36) sts. *Foundation row 1* (WS) [K1, p1] twice, p1 (0, 0, 1,

Skill Intermediate

Fit Loose

Sizes S (M, L, 1X, 2X). Shown in Large.

Finished measurements 41½ (45, 48¾, 52¾, 57½)" around, when buttoned, and 26½ (27½, 28½, 29, 29)" long.

Gauge 13 sts and 18 rows to 10cm/4" over St st (k on RS, p on WS), using size 6.5mm/US 10½ needles.

Yarn 810 (890, 990, 1070, 1150) yds. Bulky weight.

Needles Size 6.5mm/US 10½ *or size to obtain gauge.*

Buttons Four 32mm /1¼".

Extras Size 5.00mm (H/8) crochet hook.

Original yarn Tahki Soho (100% wool; 3½oz/100g; 110yds/100m).

Chart dimensions (Back and Right Front): 5¼ (6,6,6½,7¼)" · 6 (6¼,7,7¼,7½)" · 1" · 1" · 9 (9,9½,9½,10)" · 11½ (12,12,12½,12½)" · 25½ (26½,27½,28,28)" · 16½ (17½,18,18½,18)" · 15 (15½,16½,16½,16½)" · 20½ (22½,24¼,26¼,28½)" · 11 (11¾,12¾,13¾,15)"

Sleeve dimensions: 1¼ (1¾,1¾,2¼,2½)" · 18 (18,19,19,20)" · 13 (13½,14,14,14)" · 4½" · 10 (10½,11,11½,12)"

0), [k1, p1] 3 (4, 4, 4, 5) times, k2, p4, k2, p8 (9, 11, 12, 14), cast on 2 sts. *Row 2* K10 (11, 13, 14, 16), p2, k1, M1, k2, M1, k1, p2, sl 1, work row 1 of Moss st over 6 (7, 7, 8, 9) sts, [sl 1, k1] twice. *Row 3* [K1, p1] twice, work row 2 of Moss st over 6 (7, 7, 8, 9) sts, p1, k2, p6, k2, p to end, cast on 2 sts. *Begin Chart A: Row 1* (RS) K12 (13, 15, 16, 18), work 10 sts Chart A, sl 1, work Moss st as established over 6 (7, 7, 8, 9) sts, [sl 1, k1] twice. Continue in pats as established, casting on 2 sts at end of next WS row. Work 2 rows even, then inc 1 st at same edge every RS row 3 (4, 5, 6, 7) times—38 (41, 44, 47, 51) sts. Mark beginning of last inc row. Complete to correspond to right front, reversing shaping.

Sleeve Cuff *MAKE 2*

Cast on 16 sts. *Foundation row* (WS) [K1, p1] twice, [p1, k1] 6 times. *Begin pats: Row 1* (RS) [K1, sl 1] twice, work Moss st over 8 sts, [sl 1, k1] twice. *Row 2* [K1, p1] twice, work 8 sts Moss st, [p1, k1] twice. Rep last 2 rows until piece measures 10 (10½, 11, 11½, 12)" from beginning. Bind off all sts.

Right Sleeve

With RS facing, pick up and k32 (34, 36, 38, 40) sts evenly along long edge of cuff. *Foundation row 1* (WS) P12 (13, 14, 15, 16), k2, p4, k2, p to end. *Row 2* Work row 1 of Moss st over 11 (12, 13, 14, 15) sts, sl 1, p2, k1, M1, k2, M1, k1, p2, sl 1, work Moss st to end. *Row 3* Work 11 (12, 13, 14, 15) sts in Moss st, p1, k2, p6, k2, p1, work Moss st to end. *Begin Chart B: Row 1* (RS) Work 11 (12, 13, 14, 15) sts in Moss st, sl 1, work 10 sts Chart B, sl 1, work Moss st to end. Work 1 row even. Continue in pats as established, AT SAME TIME, inc 1 st each side (working incs into Moss st) on next row, then every 4th row 6 (2, 3, 0, 3) times, every 6th row 4 (7, 7, 9, 7) times—56 (56, 60, 60, 64) sts. Work even until piece measures 17½ (18, 18½, 18½, 18½)" from beginning (including cuff), end with a WS row.

Shape cap

Bind off 3 (3, 4, 4, 5) sts at beginning of next 2 rows. Dec 1 st each side every RS row 2 (3, 3, 4, 5) times—46 (44, 46, 44, 44) sts. Work 1 row even. Bind off all sts.

Left Sleeve

Work as for right sleeve, except use Chart A, instead of B.

Finishing

Block pieces. Sew shoulders. Sew front neck extensions to back neck. Sew ends tog at center back neck. Set in sleeves. Sew side seams above markers. Sew sleeve seams.

Crocheted edging

With RS facing, join yarn with crochet hook to lower left front edge and work 1 row single crochet evenly along lower edge of piece, maintaining curve at side edges. Do not turn. Work 1 row backwards single crochet. Fasten off. Work 4 chain buttonloops on right front edge as follows: Join yarn 9½ (10, 10, 10½, 10½)" down from shoulder, sl st 2, *ch 6, sl st 6; rep from* 3 times more, sl st 2. Fasten off. Sew buttons opposite loops. ∩

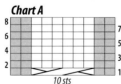

Chart B

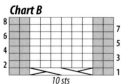

Chart A

10 sts

⬜ K on RS, p on WS

▨ P on RS, k on WS

⟋⟍ **3/3 RC** Sl 3 to cn, hold to back, k3; k3 from cn.

⟍⟋ **3/3 LC** Sl 3 to cn, hold to front, k3; k3 from cn.

sensational shirttail

outdoor ribbing

The stitch pattern on this walking jacket is reminiscent of a pine forest. Even if most of your strolling this autumn is done on city streets rather than forest paths, this relaxed outdoor knit is just right. Because the overall ribbed stitch naturally pulls in, it's a good idea to pin out your gauge swatch and cover it with a damp cloth until dry before measuring it. And do remember to block all pieces to size before sewing them together.

Katharine Hunt

outdoor ribbing

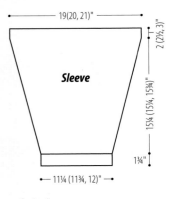

Note

Work gauge swatch as follows: With larger needles, cast on 26 sts. *Row 1* (RS) [K2, p2] 6 times, k2. *Row 2* K the knit sts and p the purl sts. *Row 3* K2, p2, work 6 sts of Chart B, rib to end. *Rows 4–10* Continue in pats through chart row 8. *Rows 11–22* Work in k2, p2 rib. *Row 23* Rib 16 sts, work 6 sts of Chart B, rib to end. *Rows 24–30* Continue in pats through chart row 8. *Rows 31–34* Work in k2, p2 rib. Piece measures approx 10cm/4" wide by 13cm/5¼" long.

Back

With smaller needles, cast on 122 (146, 170) sts. *Row 1* (RS) P2, *k2, p2; rep from* to end. Work 11 rows more in rib. Change to larger needles. *Begin Chart A:* Beginning and ending as indicated for back, work chart rows 1–26. Rib 8 rows. Work 26 rows of Chart A. *Rib 12 rows. Continue in pats as established through chart row 8. Rib 12 rows. *Begin Chart B: Row 1* (RS) Rib 10 (22, 10), [work 6 sts Chart B, rib 18] 4 (5, 6) times, [work 6 sts Chart B] 1 (0, 1) time, rib 10 (4, 10). Continue in pats as established through chart row 8. Rib 12 rows. *Begin Chart B: Row 1* (RS) Rib 22 (10, 22), [work 6 sts Chart B, rib 18] 4 (5, 6) times, [work 6 sts Chart B] 0 (1, 0) time, rib 4 (10, 4). Continue in pats as established through chart row 8. Rep from* until piece measures 16½ (17, 17½)" from beginning, end with a WS row.

Shape armholes

Note Continue Chart B above armhole shaping, lining pat up with pat below. Bind off 12 (16, 20) sts at beginning of next 2 rows—98 (114, 130) sts. Work even until armhole measures 9½ (10, 10½)", end with a WS row.

Shape shoulders

Bind off 9 (9, 11) sts at beginning of next 4 rows, 9 (9, 10) sts at beginning of next 2 rows, 0 (7, 9) sts at beginning of next 2 rows. Bind off rem 44 (46, 48) sts for back neck.

Right Front

With smaller needles, cast on 61 (73, 85) sts. *Row 1* (RS) P1, *k2, p2; rep from* to end. Work 11 rows more in rib. Change to larger needles. *Begin Chart A:* Beginning and ending as indicated for Right Front, work chart rows 1–26. Rib 8 rows. Work 26 rows Chart A. *Rib 12 rows. Continue in pats as established through chart row 8. Rib 12 rows. *Begin Chart B: Row 1* (RS) Rib 21, [work 6 sts Chart B, rib 18] 1 (1, 2) times, work 6 sts Chart B, rib 10 (22, 10). *Begin Chart B: Row 1* (RS) Rib 9, [work 6 sts Chart B, rib 18] 2 (2, 3) times, [work 6 sts Chart B] 0 (1, 0) time, rib 4 (10, 4). Continue in pats as established through chart row 8. Rep from* until piece measures same length as back to armhole. Shape armhole at beginning of WS row

as for back—49 (57, 65) sts. Work even until armhole measures 6¾ (7, 7¼)", end with a WS row.

Shape neck

Next row (RS) Bind off 8 sts (neck edge), work to end. Continue to bind off at neck edge 3 sts twice. Dec 1 st at neck edge every row 5 times, then every other row 3 (4, 5) times—27 (34, 41) sts. Work even until armhole measures same as back to shoulder. Shape shoulder at beginning of WS rows as for back.

Left Front

With smaller needles, cast on 61 (73, 85) sts. *Row 1* (RS) *P2, k2; rep from*, end p1. Work 11 rows more in rib. Change to larger needles. *Begin Chart A:* Beginning and ending as indicated for Left Front, work chart rows 1–26. Rib 8 rows. Work 26 rows Chart A. *Rib 12 rows. *Begin Chart B: Row 1* (RS) Rib 10 (22, 10), [work 6 sts Chart B, rib 18] 2 (2, 3) times, rib 3. Continue in pats as established through chart row 8. Rib 12 rows. *Begin Chart B: Row 1* (RS) Rib 22 (10, 22), [work 6 sts Chart B, rib 18] 1 (2, 2) times, work 6 sts Chart B, rib 9. Continue in pats as established through chart row 8. Rep from* and complete to correspond to right front, reversing armhole, neck and shoulder shaping.

Skill Intermediate
Fit Standard
Sizes S (M, L). Shown in Medium.
Finished measurements 39¼ (46½, 53¾)" around, when buttoned, and 27 (28¼, 29¼)" long.
Gauge 26 sts and 26 rows equal 10cm/4" over Chart B and rib, using larger needles (see note).
Yarn 1665 (1960, 2275) yds. Medium weight.
Needles Size 3.75 and 4.5mm/US 5 and 7, *or size to obtain gauge*.
Buttons Five 25mm/1".
Original yarn Patons Pure Wool Aran (100% wool; 3½oz/100g; 178yds/ 163m).

□ K on RS, p on WS

▓ P on RS, k on WS

Chart B

8   7
6   5
4   3
2   1

6 sts

2/2 RC Sl 2 to cn, hold to back, k2; k2 from cn.

2/2 LC Sl 2 to cn, hold to front, k2; k2 from cn.

2/2 RPC Sl 2 to cn, hold to back, k2; p2 from cn.

2/2 LPC Sl 2 to cn, hold to front, p2; k2 from cn.

2/2/2 RPC Sl 4 to cn, hold to back, k2; sl last 2 sts from cn back to LH needle; p2; k2 from cn.

Chart A

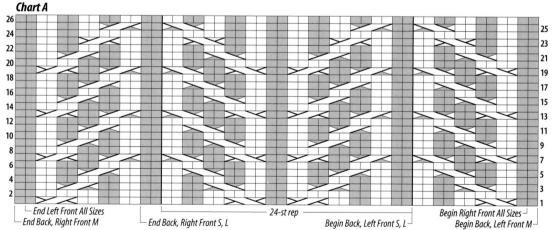

26   25
24   23
22   21
20   19
18   17
16   15
14   13
12   11
10   9
8   7
6   5
4   3
2   1

└ End Left Front All Sizes
└ End Back, Right Front M

└ End Back, Right Front S, L

── 24-st rep ──

└ Begin Back, Left Front S, L

└ Begin Right Front All Sizes ┘
└ Begin Back, Left Front M

Sleeves

Note Read through instructions before knitting sleeves.

With smaller needles, cast on 72 (74, 76) sts. *Row 1* (RS) P1 (0, 0), k2 (0, 1), *p2, k2; rep from*, end p1 (2, 2), k0 (0, 1). Work 11 rows more in rib, inc 1 st each side on last row—74 (76, 78) sts. Change to larger needles. *Begin Chart A: Row 1 (RS)* K0 (1, 2), work 24-st rep of chart 3 times, p2, k0 (1, 2). Continue pats and work shaping simultaneously as follows: *work shaping* : inc 1 st each side (working incs into rib pat) on chart row 5, then every other row 0 (4, 6) times, every 4th row 24 (22, 22) times—124 (130, 136) sts, AT SAME TIME, *work pats* : continue in Chart A as established through chart row 26. Rib 12 rows. *Begin Chart B: Row 1* (RS) Rib 19 (22, 24), [work 6 sts of Chart B, rib 18] 3 times, rib 1 (4, 6). Work through chart row 8. Rib 12 rows. *Begin Chart B: Row 1* (RS) Rib 12 (15, 17), [work 6 sts of Chart B, rib 18] 3 times, work 6 sts of Chart B, rib 12 (15, 17). Work through chart row 8. Rib 12 rows. *Begin Chart B: Row 1* (RS) Rib 5 (8, 10), [work 6 sts of Chart B, rib 18] 4 times, work 6 sts of Chart B, rib 5 (8, 10). Work through chart row 8. Rib 12 rows. *Begin Chart B: Row 1* (RS) Rib 22 (1, 3), [work 6 sts of Chart B, rib 18] 4 (5, 5) times, [work 6 sts of Chart B] 0 (1, 1) time, rib 4 (1, 3). Work through chart row 8. Continue in rib until piece measures 19 (19½, 20½)" from beginning. Bind off all sts.

Finishing

Block pieces. Sew shoulders.

Neckband

With RS facing and smaller needles, pick up and k36 (41, 46) sts along right front neck to shoulder, 44 (46, 48) sts along back neck, 36 (41, 46) sts along left front neck—116 (128, 140) sts. *Row 1* (WS) K3, *p2, k2; rep from*, end k1. Work 9 more rows in rib as established. Bind off in pat.

Buttonband

With RS facing and smaller needles, begin at top of neckband and pick up and k162 (166, 170) sts along left front edge. *Row 1* (WS) *P2, k2; rep from*, end p2. Work 9 more rows in rib as established.

Buttonhole band

Work to correspond to buttonband, working buttonholes on 5th row as follows: rib 6 (8, 10), *bind off 6 sts, rib 30; rep from* 3 times more, bind off 6 sts, rib 6 (8, 10). On next row, cast on 6 sts over each set of bound-off sts. Set in sleeves. Sew side and sleeve seams. Sew on buttons. ∩

When I began planning this project, I wanted to do something different. Cables without a cable needle and cable twists seemed ideal. The Irish Moss cardigan is a collection of twisted stitches done in various ways and a 3-stitch cable created by knitting the 3rd stitch before the 1st and 2nd stitches. Using these simple techniques I was able to create a tiny twisted braid, a simple cable, and a mock Aran diamond. Add these together and the result is an intricate appearance without the use of an extra needle.

Nancy Bush

Irish moss

Notes

1 See *School*, p. 102, for ssk, sssk, Make 1 (M1 and M1P), and 3-needle bind-off.
2 First and last st of every row on every piece are worked in St st including during shaping.

Moss Stitch

Row 1 (RS) *P1, k1; rep from *. *Rows 2 and 4* K the knit sts and p the purl sts. *Row 3* *K1, p1; rep from*.

Back

With smaller needles, cast on 117 (122, 132) sts. [Work Chart A rows 1–4] 3 (3, 4) times, then work rows 1–2 once. Piece measures approx 2 (2, 3)". *Next row* (WS) Change to larger needles and knit, inc 12 (15, 21) sts evenly across—129 (137, 153) sts. Work Chart B rows 1–4, inc 1 (1, 0) sts on last row—130 (138, 153) sts. *Next row* (RS) K1, work 1 (5, 1) sts Moss St, [work Chart C over 11 sts, work Chart D over 12 sts] 5 (5, 6) times, work Chart C over 11 sts, work 1 (5, 1) sts Moss st, k1. Continue in pat as established until piece measures 14 (14½, 15½)" from beginning, end with a WS row.

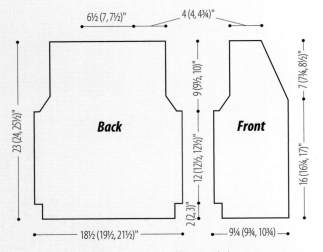

Shape armholes

Bind off 5 sts at beginning of next 2 rows. *Next (dec) row* K1, ssk, work to last 3 sts in pat, k2tog, k1. *Next row* P2, work in pat to last 2 sts, p2. Rep last 2 rows 7 (8, 8) times more—104 (110, 125) sts. Work even until armhole measures 9 (9½, 10)", end with a WS row. Place sts on hold.

Right Front

With smaller needles, cast on 57 (62, 67) sts. Work Chart A as for back until 14 (14, 18) rows completed. *Next row* (WS) Change to larger needles and knit, inc 8

Left column info

Skill Intermediate
Fit Standard
Sizes S (M, L). Shown in Medium.
Finished measurements 38 (40, 44)" around, when buttoned, and 23 (24, 25½)" long.
Gauge 20 sts and 22 rows equal 10cm/4" over Moss st, using larger needles.
Yarn 1550 (1680, 1940) yds. Medium weight.
Needles Size 3.25 and 3.75mm/US 3 and 5, *or size needed to obtain gauge*.
Buttons 6 (6, 7) 19mm/¾" buttons.
Extras Stitch holders.
Original yarn Bryspun Kid n' Ewe (50% wool, 50% mohair; 1¾oz/50g; 120 yds/110m).

Chart legend

☐ K on RS, p on WS
▨ P on RS, k on WS
◨ K 1 through back loop (tbl)
◯ Yarn over
╱ K2tog

⟋⟍ **1/1 RT** On RS: K2tog, then k first st only again and slip both sts off needle. On WS: P 2nd st, then p first st, slip both sts off needle.

⟍⟋ **1/1 LT** K 2nd st through back loop (tbl), then k first st, slip both sts off needle.

⟍⟋ **1/1 LT tbl** K 2nd st through back loop (tbl), then k first and 2nd sts tog tbl, slip both sts off needle.

⟋⟋ **1/2 RC** K 3rd st (through front), k first st tbl, then k 2nd st tbl; sl all 3 sts off needle.

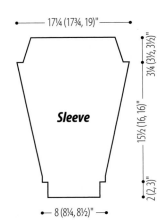

Chart A — 5-st rep

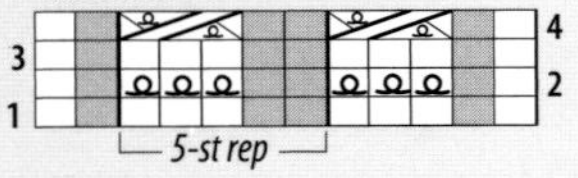

Chart B — 2-st rep

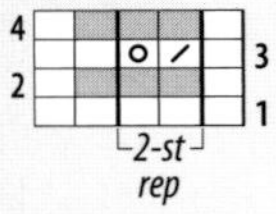

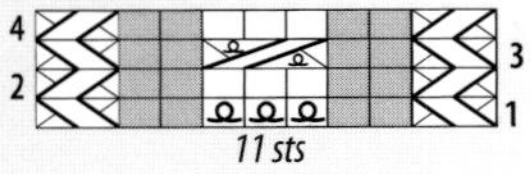

Chart C — 11 sts

Chart D — 12 sts

Back Pat Arrangement

1 st St st	1 (5, 1) sts Moss st	11 sts Chart C	12 sts Chart D	11 sts Chart C	1 (5, 1) sts Moss st	1 st St st
			5 (5, 6)x			

Right Front Pat Arrangement

1 st St st	1 (5, 1) sts Moss st	11 sts Chart C	12 sts Chart D	11 sts Chart C	6 sts Moss st	1 st St st
		1 (1, 0)x	2 (2, 3)x			

Left Front Pat Arrangement

1 st St st	6 sts Moss st	11 sts Chart C	12 sts Chart D	11 sts Chart C	1 (5, 1) sts Moss st	1 st St st
		2 (2, 3)x	1 (1, 0)x			

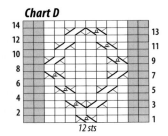

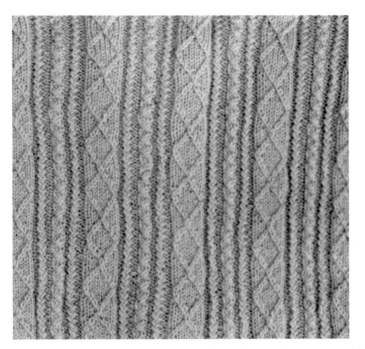

(7, 10) sts evenly across— 65 (69, 77) sts. Work Chart B rows 1–4, inc 1 st on last row—66 (70, 78) sts. *Next row* (RS) K1, work 6 sts Moss St, [work Chart C, work Chart D] 2 (2, 3) times, work Chart C 1 (1, 0) times, work 1 (5, 1) sts Moss st, k1. Work same as Back until piece is same length as Back to armhole.

Shape armhole and V-neck

Shape armhole as for Back at beginning of WS rows, AT SAME TIME, when piece measures 16 (16¼, 17)" from beginning, ending with a WS row, begin V-neck shaping as follows: *Next row* (RS) K1, sssk, work to end. Rep last row every RS row 9 times more, then work every RS row as k1, ssk, work to end 6 (8, 10) times—27 (28, 34) sts. Work even until Front is same length as Back. Place sts on hold.

Left Front

Work as for Right Front to 66 (70, 78) sts. *Next row* (RS) K1, work 1 (5, 1) sts Moss St, work Chart C 1 (1, 0) times, [work Chart D, work Chart C] 2 (2, 3) times, work 6 sts Moss St, k1. Work as for Right Front, shaping armhole at beginning of RS rows, and shaping neckline at end of RS rows working first 10 dec rows as follows: work to last 4 sts, k3tog, k1. Work remaining dec rows by working to last 3 sts, k2tog, k1.

Sleeves

With smaller needles, cast on 52 (57, 57) sts. Work rows 1–14 (14, 18) as for Back. *Next row* (WS) Change to larger needles and knit, inc 7 (4, 6) sts evenly across— 59 (61, 63) sts. Work Chart B rows 1–4, inc 1 st on last row—60 (62, 64) sts. *Note* Work incs after first and before last st as either M1 or M1P as required for the Moss St.

Next row (RS) K1, work 0 (1, 2) sts Moss St, [work Chart D, work Chart C] 2 times, work Chart D, work 0 (1, 2) sts Moss St, k1. Continue in pat, inc 1 st each side (into Moss St) on row 3 then every other row 9 (10, 16) times more, then every 4th row 14 (14, 11) times—108 (112, 120) sts. Work even until piece measures 17½ (18, 19)", end with a WS row. Shape armhole as for Back, binding off 82 (84, 92) sts on first RS row after dec completed.

Finishing

Join shoulders using 3-needle bind-off and leaving center Back 50 (54, 57) sts on hold.

Right Front Band

With RS facing and smaller needles, pick up and k87 (87, 92) sts along Right Front to beginning of V-neck shaping. Work Chart A Rows 1–2. *Row 3* (WS) Work 5 sts, bind off 2 sts, [work until 13 sts after bound off 2 on needle, bind off 2 sts] 5 (5, 4) times, [work to 8 sts after bound-off 2, bind-off 2 sts] 0 (0, 2) times, work to end. Work Row 4 casting on 2 sts over bound-off sts. Work Rows 1–3. Bind off all sts.

Left Front Band

Work as for Right Front Band, begin pick up at neck shaping and working down to lower edge and omitting buttonholes.

Collar

Place 50 (54, 57) sts from Back neck holder on smaller needle ready for a RS row (will become WS of collar). *Row 1* Work Moss St, dec 1 (1, 0) sts at center, then pick up and k2 sts along Left neck edge—51 (55, 59) sts. *Row 2* Work Moss St, then pick up and p2 sts along Right neck edge. *Row 3* Work Moss St, then pick up and k2 sts along Left neck edge. Rep last 2 rows, ending with row 2, until the center edge of each front band has been reached. *Note* Be sure to pick up evenly along each neck edge so that the center is reached on both sides at the same time. Bind off loosely in pat.

Sew in tops of sleeves, matching center of middle diamond to shoulder seam. Sew side and sleeve seams. Sew on buttons. ∩

Irish moss

simply shawled

This jacket is designed to flatter many sizes, including larger ones. The wide vertical traveling cable panels are attractive while not adding bulk to the garment.

Gitta Schrade

simply shawled

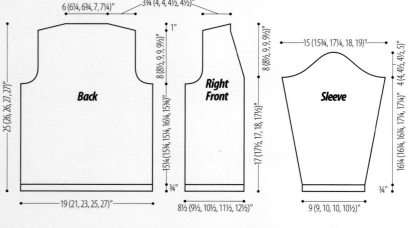

Seed st

Row 1 (RS)*K1, p1; rep from*. *Row 2* K the purl sts and p the knit sts. Rep row 2 for Seed st.

Pat st

Work 12 rows in St st, 6 rows in Seed st; rep from (18 rows) for Pat st.

Back

With smaller needles, cast on 108 (118, 128, 138, 148) sts. Work 6 rows in Seed st. Change to larger needles. *Begin Pat st and Charts A and B: Row 1* (RS) Work 17 (21, 24, 29, 32) sts in Pat st, 26 sts of Chart A, 22 (24, 28, 28, 32) sts in Pat st, 26 sts of Chart B, 17 (21, 24, 29, 32) sts in Pat st. Continue in pats as established until piece measures 16 (16½, 16, 17, 16½)" from beginning, end with a WS row.

Shape armholes

Continue pats, bind off 4 (7, 8, 9, 10) sts at beginning of next 2 rows, 2 sts at beginning of next 4 (4, 6, 8, 10) rows. Dec 1 st each side on next row, then every other row 5 times more—80 (84, 88, 92, 96) sts. Work even until armhole measures 8 (8½, 9, 9, 9½)", end with a WS row.

Shape shoulders

Bind off 8 (9, 8, 9, 9) sts at beginning of next 2 rows, 8 (8, 9, 9, 10) sts at beginning of next 4 rows. Bind off rem 32 (34, 36, 38, 38) sts.

Right Front

With smaller needles, cast on 49 (54, 59, 64, 69) sts. Work 6 rows in Seed st. Change to larger needles. *Begin Pat st and Chart B: Row 1* (RS) Work 6 (7, 9, 9, 11) sts in Pat st, 26 sts of Chart B, 17 (21, 24, 29, 32) sts in Pat st. Continue in pats as established until same length as back to underarm.

Shape armhole and V-neck

Shape armhole at side edge as for back, AT SAME TIME, when armhole measures 1", end with a WS row and shape V-neck as follows: Dec 1 st at neck edge on next row, then every 4th row 10 (11, 12, 13, 13) times more—24 (25, 26, 27, 29) sts. When armhole measures same length as back to shoulder, shape shoulder as for back.

Left Front

Work as for right front, reversing pats and shaping. *Begin Pat st and Chart A: Row 1* (RS) Work 17 (21, 24, 29, 32) sts in Pat st, 26 sts of Chart A, 6 (7, 9, 9, 11) sts in Pat st.

Sleeves

With smaller needles, cast on 45 (45, 50, 50, 53) sts. Work 6 rows in Seed st. Continue in Seed st, AT SAME TIME, inc 1 st each side (working incs into pat) on next

row, then every 8th (8th, 8th, 6th, 6th) row 1 (9, 14, 3, 7) times, every 10th (10th, 10th, 8th, 8th) row 13 (7, 3, 16, 13) times—75 (79, 86, 90, 95) sts. Work even until piece measures 17 (17½, 17½, 18, 18)" from beginning, end with a WS row.

Shape cap

Bind off 4 (7, 8, 9, 10) sts at beginning of next 2 rows. Dec 1 st each side on next row, then every other row 12 (14, 16, 15, 19) times more, then every row 5 (1, 1, 3, 1) times. Bind off 5 sts at beginning of next 4 rows. Bind off rem 11 (13, 14, 14, 13) sts.

Finishing

Block pieces. Sew shoulders.

Front bands and collar

(*Note* Work buttonhole on a RS row as follows: Work 5 sts, bind off 3 sts, work 5 sts. On next row, cast on 3 sts over bound-off sts.)

With smaller needles, cast on 13 sts. Work in Seed st until band, slightly stretched, fits along left front edge to beginning of neck shaping, place marker (pm). Place markers for 6 buttons on band, with the first 3 rows down from needle, the last ¾" from lower edge, and 4 others spaced evenly between. Continue in Seed st, AT SAME TIME, inc 1 st at neck edge (beginning of every RS row) 30 (31, 34, 37, 40) times—43 (44, 47, 50, 53) sts, pm for end of shaping. Work even until piece fits (without stretching) to shoulder, pm. Work even until piece fits to center back neck, pm, work to shoulder, pm, work even until same length as first half to shaping marker. Work decs at neck edge to correspond to incs of first half, end at beginning of neck shaping—13 sts. Pm, then continue in Seed st, working buttonholes opposite markers, until piece fits to lower edge. Bind off all sts in pat. Set in sleeves. Sew side and sleeve seams. Sew front bands and collar in place, using markers as a guide to placement. Sew on buttons. ∩

Skill Intermediate
Fit Standard
Sizes S (M, L, 1X, 2X). Shown in Small.
Finished measurements 38 (42, 46, 50, 54)" around, when buttoned, and 25 (26, 26, 27, 27)" long.
Gauge 20 sts and 26 rows equal 10cm/4" over St st (k on RS, p on WS), using larger needles.
20 sts and 36 rows equal 10cm/4" over Seed st, using smaller needles.
Yarn 1830 (2055, 2255, 2500, 2680) yds. Medium weight.
Needles Size 4 and 4.5mm/US 6 and 7, *or size to obtain gauge.*
Buttons Six 25mm/1".
Extras Cable needle (cn). Stitch markers.
Original yarn SR Kertzer Aspiring, Aran 10 Ply (60% wool, 40% alpaca; 3½oz/100g; 183yds/165m)

Chart A

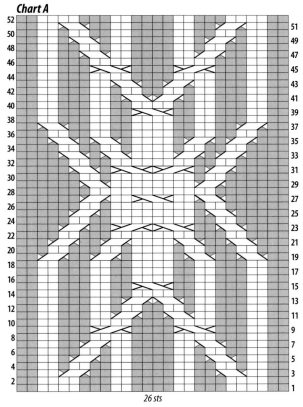

26 sts

CHART B *(over 26 sts)*

Work as for chart A, except work 2/2 RC, instead of 2/2 LC, over center 4 sts on rows 15, 27, and 39. See close-up photo.

☐ K on RS, p on WS

▨ P on RS, k on WS

2/1 RPC Sl 1 to cn, hold to back, k2; p1 from cn.

2/1 LPC Sl 2 to cn, hold to front, p1; k2 from cn.

2/2 RC Sl 2 to cn, hold to back, k2; k2 from cn.

2/2 LC Sl 2 to cn, hold to front, k2; k2 from cn.

In my design process I like to have things flow so that everything in a sweater looks complementary. I have always been interested in textures and have a large collection of ribbings. My main focus in this cardigan was the bobble. I had a bobble ribbing and changed one of the cable patterns in the body of the sweater to use the same bobble.

Kathy Zimmerman

bobbled braids

Note

1 See *School*, p. 102, for Make 1 (M1), ssk, ssp, and 3-needle bind-off. **2** Make 1 knit is abbreviated (M1K), and Make 1 purl is abbreviated (M1P).

Make Bobble (MB) [P1, k1] twice into next st, pass the first three sts, one at a time, over the 4th st.

Back

With smaller needles, cast on 133 (137, 143, 155) sts. *Begin Chart A: Row 1* (WS) Begin as indicated for your size, and reading chart from left to right, work to beginning of 8-st rep, then work rep across to last 0 (2, 5, 3) sts, end as indicated. Continue in pat as established until 4 rows of chart have been worked 2 (2, 3, 3) times, then work rows 1-3 once more. Ribbing measures approx 2 (2, 2½, 2½)". Change to larger needles. *Foundation row* (RS) *Size S* P2, *k1, p2, k2, p10, k2, M1K, k1, p10, k2, p2, k1**, p1, p2tog, k9, p2tog, p1; rep from*, end last rep at**, p2—132 sts. *Size M* K2, p2, *k1, p2, k2, p10, k2, M1K, k1, p10, k2, p2, k1, p2**, p1, k9, p3; rep from*, end last rep at**, k2—140 sts. *Size L* P7, *k1, p2, M1P, k2, p10, k2, M1K, k1, p10, k2, M1P, p2, k1, p3**, k9, p3; rep from*, end last rep at**, p4—152 sts. *Size 1X* P1, M1P, p1, M1K, k8, p3, *k1, p2, k2, p10, k2, M1K, k1, p10, k2, p2, k1, p3**, k9, p3; rep from*, end last rep at**, k8, M1K, p1, M1P, p1—162 sts.

Begin Charts B, C, and D: Row 1 (WS) P0 (2, 3, 0), k0 (0, 2, 2), work 0 (0, 0, 11) sts of Chart D, [5 sts Chart B, 28 (28, 30, 28) sts Chart C, 5 sts Chart B, 9 (11, 11, 11) sts Chart D] twice, 5 sts Chart B, 28 (28, 30, 28) sts Chart C, 5 sts Chart B, 0 (0, 0, 11) sts Chart D, k0 (0, 2, 2), p0 (2, 3, 0). Continue in pats as established until piece measure 24 (25, 26, 27)" from beginning, end with a WS row.

Shape neck

Next row (RS) Work in pat across 46 (48, 54, 58) sts, join 2nd ball of yarn and bind off center 40 (44, 44, 46) sts, work to end. Working both sides at same time, bind off from each neck edge 2 sts once, then 1 st once—43 (45, 51, 55) sts each side. Work even until piece measures 25 (26, 27, 28)" from beginning. Place sts on hold.

Right Front

With smaller needles, cast on 69 (71, 74, 80) sts. *Begin Chart A: Row 1* (WS) Begin as indicated for your size, and reading chart from left to right, work to beginning of 8-st rep, then work rep across to end. Continue in pat as established to match back

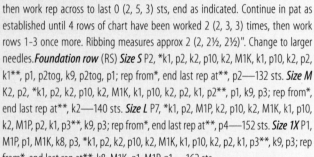

ribbing. Change to larger needles. *Foundation row* (RS) *Size S* P2, [k1, p1, p2tog, k9, p2tog, p1] twice, k1, p2, k2, p10, k2, M1K, k1, p10, k2, p2, k1, p2—66 sts. *Size M* P2, [k1, p3, k9, p3] twice, k1, p2, k2, p10, k2, M1K, k1, p10, k2, p2, k1, p2, k2—72 sts. *Size L* P2, [k1, p3, k9, p3] twice, k1, p2, M1P, k2, p10, k2, M1K, k1, p10, k2, M1P, p2, k1, p7—77 sts. *Size 1X* P2, [k1, p3, k9, p3] twice, k1, p2, k2, p10, k2, M1K, k1, p10, k2, p2, k1, p3, k8, M1K, p1, M1P, p1—83 sts.

Begin Charts B, C, and D: Row 1 (WS) P0 (2, 3, 0), k0 (0, 2, 2), work 0 (0, 0, 11) sts Chart D, 5 sts Chart B, 28 (28, 30, 28) sts Chart C, 5 sts Chart B, [9 (11, 11, 11) sts Chart D, 5 sts Chart B] twice. Continue in pats as established until piece measures 18 (19, 19, 20)" from beginning, end with a WS row.

Shape V-neck

Dec 1 st at neck edge (ssk on RS, ssp on WS) every row 3 (7, 4, 6) times, then every other row 20 (20, 22, 22) times—43 (45, 51, 55) sts. Work even until piece measures same length as back to shoulder. Place sts on hold.

Left Front

Work to correspond to right front, reversing pats and shaping. *Begin Chart A: Row 1* (WS) Begin as indicated for your size, and reading chart from left to right, work to beginning of 8-st rep, then work rep across to last 0 (2, 5, 3) sts, end as indicated. *Foundation row* (RS) *Size S* P2, k1, p2, k2, p10, k2, M1K, k1, p10, k2, p2, k1, [p1, p2tog, k9, p2tog, p1, k1] twice, p2—66 sts. *Size M* K2, p2, k1, p2, k2, p10, k2, M1K, k1, p10, k2, p2, k1, [p3, k9, p3, k1] twice, p2—72 sts. *Size L* P7, k1, p2, M1P, k2, p10, k2, M1K, k1, p10, k2, M1P, p2, k1, [p3, k9, p3, k1] twice, p2—77 sts. *Size 1X* P1, M1P, p1, M1K, k8, p3, k1, p2, k2, p10, k2, M1K, k1, p10, k2, p2, k1, [p3, k9, p3, k1] twice, p2—83 sts.

Skill Intermediate
Fit Standard
Sizes S (M, L, 1X). Shown in Medium.
Finished measurements 38 (42, 46, 50)" around, when buttoned, and 25 (26, 27, 28)" long.
Gauge 21 sts and 28 rows equal 10cm/4" in St st (k on RS, p on WS) with larger needles. 28 sts of Chart C equal 9.5cm/3¾"; 9 sts of Chart D equal 3.8cm/1½".
Yarn 1950 (2200, 2475, 2730) yds. Medium weight.
Needles Sizes 3.75 and 4.5mm/US 5 and 7, *or size to obtain gauge.* Size 4mm/US 6 circular (for neckband) 72cm/29" long.
Buttons 7 (7, 8, 8) 20 mm/¾".
Extras Cable needle (cn).
Original yarn Cascade Yarns Cascade 220 (100% wool; 3½ oz/100g; 220 yds/200m).

Begin Charts B, C, and D: Row 1 (WS) [Work 5 sts Chart B, 9 (11, 11, 11) sts Chart D] twice, 5 sts Chart B, 28 (28, 30, 28) sts Chart C, 5 sts Chart B, 0 (0, 0, 11) sts Chart D, k0 (0, 2, 2), p0 (2, 3, 0). Shape V-neck by working k2tog on RS rows, p2tog on WS rows.

Sleeves

With smaller needles, cast on 63 (63, 69, 69) sts. *Begin Chart A: Row 1* (WS) Begin as indicated for your size, and reading chart from left to right, work to beginning of 8-st rep, then work rep across to last 5 (5, 0, 0) sts, end as indicated. Continue in pat as established to match back ribbing. Change to larger needles. *Foundation row* (RS) *Sizes S, M* P1, M1P, k1, M1P, p1, M1P, k9, p3, k1, p2, k2, p10, k2, M1K, k1, p10, k2, p2, k1, p3, k9, M1P, p1, M1P, k1, M1P, p1—70 sts. *Sizes L, 1X* P2, k1, p3, k9, p3, k1, p2, k2, p10, k2, M1K, k1, p10, k2, p2, k1, p3, k9, p3, k1, p2—70 sts.

Begin Charts B, C, and D: Row 1 (WS) Work 5 sts Chart B, 11 sts Chart D, 5 sts Chart B, 28 sts Chart C, 5 sts Chart B, 11 sts Chart D, 5 sts Chart B. Continue in pats as established, AT SAME TIME, inc 1 st each side (working incs into rev St st) every 4th row 10 (16, 22, 29) times, then every 6th row 12 (9, 5, 1) times—114 (120,

124, 130) sts. Work even until piece measures 18 (19, 19½, 20)" from beginning. Bind off.

Neckband

With RS facing and circular needle, pick up and k104 (104, 112, 112) sts along right front edge to beg of V-shaping, place marker (pm), pick up and k1, pm, pick up and k141 (141, 157, 157) sts along front and back neck edges between V-shaping points, pm, pick up and k1, pm, pick up and k104 (104, 112, 112) sts along left front edge—351 (351, 383, 383) sts. *Row 1* (WS) [P3, k2, p1, k2] 13 (13, 14, 14) times, remove marker (rm), [k1, p1, k1] into next st, rm, k2, p1, k2, [p3, k2, p1, k2] 17 (17, 19, 19) times, rm, [k1, p1, k1] into next st, rm, [k2, p1, k2, p3] 13 (13, 14, 14) times. *Row 2* *K3, p2, MB, p2; rep from*, end k3. *Row 3* *P3, k2, p1, k2; rep from*, end p3. Place 7 (7, 8, 8) markers on right front for buttonholes. *Row 4* *K3, p2, k1, p2; rep from*, end k3, AT SAME TIME, work yo, k2tog buttonholes at markers. Continue in bobble rib as established until band measures 1". Bind off.

Finishing

Block pieces. Join shoulders, using 3-needle bind-off. Place markers 9½ (10, 10½, 11)" down from shoulders on front and back for armholes. Sew top of sleeves between markers. Sew side and sleeve seams. Sew on buttons.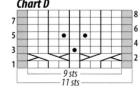

Legend

☐ K on RS, p on WS
▨ P on RS, k on WS
⊡ **MB** [P1, k1] twice into next st, pass the first 3 sts, one at a time, over the 4th st.

⟋ **2/1 RC** Sl 1 to cn, hold to back, k2; k1 from cn.

⟍ **2/1 LC** Sl 2 to cn, hold to front, k1; k2 from cn.

⟋ **2/1 RPC** Sl 1 to cn, hold to back, k2; p1 from cn.

⟍ **2/1 LPC** Sl 2 to cn, hold to front, p1; k2 from cn.

⟋ **2/2 RC** Sl 2 to cn, hold to back, k2; k2 from cn.

⟍ **2/2 LC** Sl 2 to cn, hold to front, k2; k2 from cn.

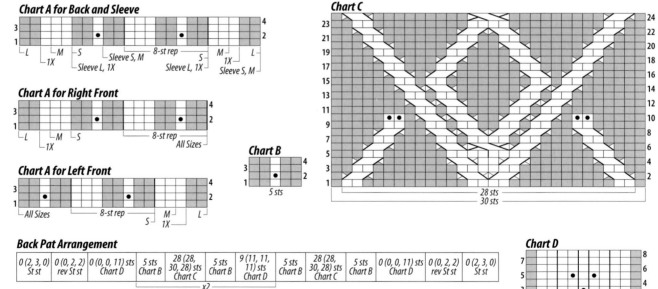

Chart A for Back and Sleeve

Chart A for Right Front

Chart A for Left Front

Chart B

Chart C

Chart D

Back Pat Arrangement

0 (2, 3, 0) St st	0 (0, 2, 2) rev St st	0 (0, 0, 11) sts Chart D	5 sts Chart B	28 (28, 30, 28) sts Chart C	5 sts Chart B	9 (11, 11, 11) sts Chart D	5 sts Chart B	28 (28, 30, 28) sts Chart C	5 sts Chart B	0 (0, 0, 11) sts Chart D	0 (0, 2, 2) rev St st	0 (2, 3, 0) St st
						x2						

Right Front Pat Arrangement

0 (2, 3, 0) St st	0 (0, 2, 2) rev St st	0 (0, 0, 11) sts Chart D	5 sts Chart B	28 (28, 30, 28) sts Chart C	5 sts Chart B	9 (11, 11, 11) sts Chart D	5 sts Chart B
						x2	

Left Front Pat Arrangement

5 sts Chart B	9 (11, 11, 11) sts Chart D	5 sts Chart B	28 (28, 30, 28) sts Chart C	5 sts Chart B	0 (0, 0, 11) sts Chart D	0 (0, 2, 2) rev St st	0 (2, 3, 0) St st
	x2						

Sleeve Pat Arrangement

5 sts Chart B	11 sts Chart D	5 sts Chart B	28 sts Chart C	5 sts Chart B	11 sts Chart D	5 sts Chart B

bobbled braids

refined Aran

Ribbing is primarily a functional device which provides shape at the sweater's lower edges. But it also has decorative potential. When planning your garment, consider the many possibilities for relating the ribbed edge to the pattern stitch above it or modifying a basic rib to enhance the overall design. The result will be a more sophisticated and better integrated garment design. In this vest, the rib border relates to the main patterns by carrying the smaller cables straight down or by adapting the components of the larger ones.

Charlotte Morris

refined Aran

Notes

1 See *School*, p. 102 for ssk, ssp, lifted inc (right and left) and 3-needle bind-off.
2 For ease in working, use markers to separate chart pats. **3** Cable pats consist of 4 parts: 2 Foundation rows, Border rep, Transition and Main Pat rep. For some pats, parts are combined into one pat. **4** Work selvage sts in garter st.

Back

With size 2.25mm (US 1) needles, cast on 174 (186, 196, 208) sts. *Begin Chart pats: Foundation row 1* (RS) K1 (selvage st), work 17 (21, 23, 29) sts Pat 1, 7 sts Pat 2A, 3 sts Pat 3, p0 (1, 1, 1) (rev St st), 6 sts Pat 4A, p0 (1, 1, 1) (rev St st), 3 sts Pat 3, 7 sts Pat 2A, p0 (0, 1, 1) (rev St st), 18 sts Pat 5A, p0 (0, 1, 1) (rev St st), 8 sts Pat 6A, p0 (0, 1, 1) (rev St st), 34 sts Pat 7, p0 (0, 1, 1) (rev St st), 8 sts Pat 6B, p0 (0, 1, 1) (rev St st), 18 sts Pat 5B, p0 (0, 1, 1) (rev St st), 7 sts Pat 2B, 3 sts Pat 3, p0 (1, 1, 1) (rev St st), 6 sts Pat 4B, p0 (1, 1, 1) (rev St st), 3 sts Pat 3, 7 sts Pat 2B, 17 (21, 23, 29) sts Pat 1, k1 (selvage st). *Row 2* Work Foundation row 2 in established pat. Work Border Rep Chart for all pats for 27 (27, 31, 31) rows more. Change to size 2.75mm (US 2) needles. *Next row* (WS) Continue Pats 2A, 2B, 3, 6A, 6B and

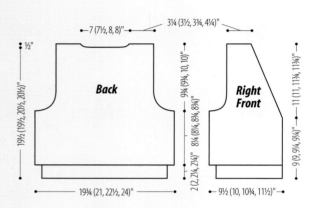

7 as set; work row 1 of Transition Chart for Pats 1, 4A, 4B, 5A and 5B. *Next row* (RS) Work row 1 of Transition Chart for Pat 7, working all other pats as set. Work through row 5 of Transition Charts for Pats 4A and 4B. *Next row* (RS) Begin Main Pat Rep Chart for Pats 4A and 4B. Work 1 row even. *Next row* (RS) Begin Main Pat Rep Chart for Pats 5A and 5B. Work through row 10 of Transition Chart for Pat 7. Change to size 3.25mm (US 3) needles. *Next row* (RS) Begin Main Pat Rep for Pat 7. All main pats are now established—194 (206, 216, 228) sts. Work even until piece measures 10¼ (10¼, 11, 11)" from beginning, end with a WS row.

Skill Experienced
Fit Standard
Sizes S (M, L, 1X). Shown in Medium.
Finished Measurements 39½ (42, 45, 48)" around, when buttoned, and 20 (20, 21, 21)" long.
Gauge 28 sts and 44 rows equal 10cm/4" over main pat rep of Pat 1 using size 3.25mm/US 3 needles.
Yarns 1140 (1210, 1360, 1455) yds. Fine weight.
Needles Sizes 2.25, 2.75, 3.25/ US 1, 2, and 3, *or size to obtain gauge*. Size 2.25mm/US 1 circular, 80cm/32" long.
Buttons Eight 15mm/⅝".
Extras Cable needle (cn). Stitch holders & markers.
Original yarn Rowan Lightweight Donegal Tweed (100% wool; ¾oz/ 25g; 110 yds (100m).

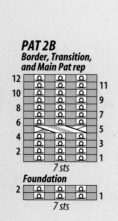

PAT 2B
Border, Transition, and Main Pat rep

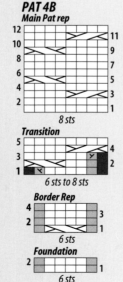

PAT 4B
Main Pat rep

Transition

6 sts to 8 sts

Border Rep

6 sts

Foundation

6 sts

7 sts

Foundation

7 sts

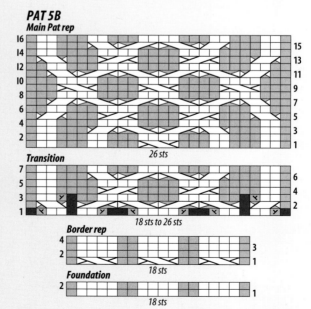

PAT 5B
Main Pat rep

26 sts

Transition

18 sts to 26 sts

Border rep

18 sts

Foundation

18 sts

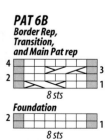

PAT 6B
Border Rep, Transition, and Main Pat rep

8 sts

Foundation

8 sts

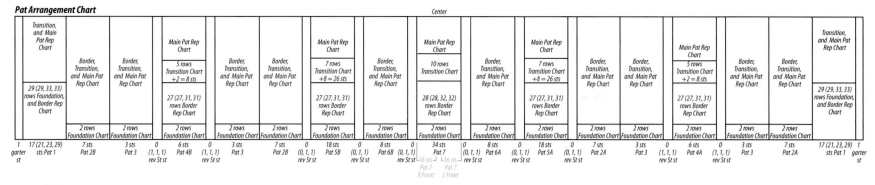

Pat Arrangement Chart

Center

Transition, and Main Pat Rep Chart			Main Pat Rep Chart			Main Pat Rep Chart		Main Pat Rep Chart		Main Pat Rep Chart				Main Pat Rep Chart			Transition, and Main Pat Rep Chart
	Border, Transition, and Main Pat Rep Chart	Border, Transition, and Main Pat Rep Chart	5 rows Transition Chart +2 = 8 sts	Border, Transition, and Main Pat Rep Chart	Border, Transition, and Main Pat Rep Chart	7 rows Transition Chart +8 = 26 sts	Border, Transition, and Main Pat Rep Chart	10 rows Transition Chart	Border, Transition, and Main Pat Rep Chart	7 rows Transition Chart +8 = 26 sts	Border, Transition, and Main Pat Rep Chart	Border, Transition, and Main Pat Rep Chart	5 rows Transition Chart +2 = 8 sts	Border, Transition, and Main Pat Rep Chart	Border, Transition, and Main Pat Rep Chart	
29 (29, 33, 33) rows Foundation, and Border Rep Chart	27 (27, 31, 31) rows Border Rep Chart					27 (27, 31, 31) rows Border Rep Chart		28 (28, 32, 32) rows Border Rep Chart		27 (27, 31, 31) rows Border Rep Chart				27 (27, 31, 31) rows Border Rep Chart			29 (29, 33, 33) rows Foundation, and Border Rep Chart
	2 rows Foundation Chart	2 rows Foundation Chart	2 rows Foundation Chart	2 rows Foundation Chart	2 rows Foundation Chart	2 rows Foundation Chart	2 rows Foundation Chart	2 rows Foundation Chart	2 rows Foundation Chart	2 rows Foundation Chart	2 rows Foundation Chart	2 rows Foundation Chart	2 rows Foundation Chart	2 rows Foundation Chart	2 rows Foundation Chart		

| 1 garter st | 17 (21, 23, 29) sts Pat 1 | 7 sts Pat 2B | 3 sts Pat 3 | 0 (1, 1, 1) rev St st | 6 sts Pat 4B | 0 (1, 1, 1) rev St st | 3 sts Pat 3 | 7 sts Pat 2B | 0 (0, 1, 1) rev St st | 18 sts Pat 5B | 0 (0, 1, 1) rev St st | 8 sts Pat 6B | 0 (0, 1, 1) rev St st [26 sts Pat 7 R Front] [16 sts Pat 7 L Front] | 34 sts Pat 7 | 0 (0, 1, 1) rev St st | 8 sts Pat 6A | 0 (0, 1, 1) rev St st | 18 sts Pat 5A | 0 (0, 1, 1) rev St st | 7 sts Pat 2A | 3 sts Pat 3 | 0 (1, 1, 1) rev St st | 6 sts Pat 4A | 0 (1, 1, 1) rev St st | 3 sts Pat 3 | 7 sts Pat 2A | 17 (21, 23, 29) sts Pat 1 | 1 garter st |

PAT 7 Main Pat rep

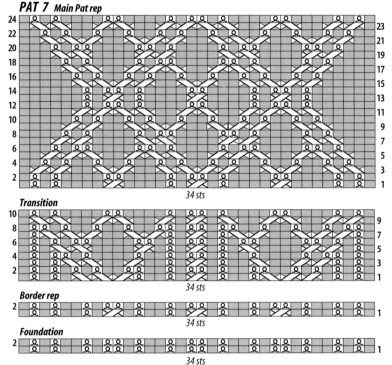

24 23 22 21 20 19 18 17 16 15 14 13 12 11 10 9 8 7 6 5 4 3 2 1
34 sts

Transition

10 9 8 7 6 5 4 3 2 1
34 sts

Border rep

2 1
34 sts

Foundation

2 1
34 sts

☐ **K on RS, p on WS**

▨ **P on RS, k on WS**

Ⓠ **K1 through back loop (tbl) on RS, p1 tbl on WS.**

∩ **K1 in row below**

☒ **Right lifted inc on WS**

☒ **Left lifted inc on WS**

∨ **Slip 1 purl-wise with yarn at WS**

W RS WRAP With yarn at WS, sl 1; with yarn at RS, sl same st back to LH needle, turn.

W WS WRAP With yarn at WS, sl 1; with yarn at RS, sl same st back to LH needle, turn.

◣ **Ssp on WS**

◿ **P2tog on WS**

◣ **Ssk on WS**

◿ **K2tog on WS**

■ **No sts exist in these areas of charts.**

1/1 RC Sl 1 to cn, hold to back, k1 tbl; k1 tbl from cn.

1/1 LC Sl 1 to cn, hold to front, k1 tbl; k1 tbl from cn.

1/1 RPC Sl 1 to cn, hold to back, k1 tbl; p1 from cn.

1/1 LPC Sl 1 to cn, hold to front, p1; k1 tbl from cn.

2/1 RPC Sl 1 to cn, hold to back, k2; p1 from cn.

2/1 LPC Sl 2 to cn, hold to front, p1; k2 from cn.

2/2 RC Sl 2 to cn, hold to back, k2; k2 from cn.

2/2 LC Sl 2 to cn, hold to front, k2; k2 from cn.

2/2 RPC Sl 2 to cn, hold to back, k2; p2 from cn.

2/2 LPC Sl 2 to cn, hold to front, p2; k2 from cn.

3/2 RPC Sl 2 to cn, hold to back, k1 tbl, p1, k1 tbl; p1, k1 tbl from cn.

3/2 LPC Sl 3 to cn, hold to front, k1 tbl, p1; k1 tbl, p1, k1 tbl from cn.

PAT 5A
Main Pat rep

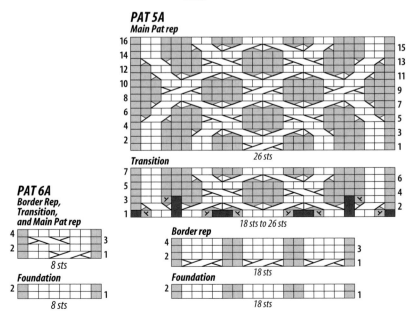

16 15 14 13 12 11 10 9 8 7 6 5 4 3 2 1
26 sts

Transition

7 6 5 4 3 2 1
18 sts to 26 sts

Border rep

4 3 2 1
18 sts

Foundation

2 1
18 sts

PAT 6A
Border Rep, Transition, and Main Pat rep

4 3 2 1
8 sts

Foundation

2 1
8 sts

PAT 4A
Main Pat rep

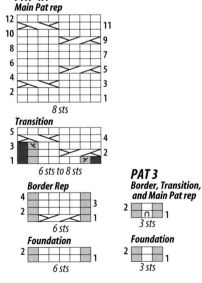

12 11 10 9 8 7 6 5 4 3 2 1
8 sts

Transition

5 4 3 2 1
6 sts to 8 sts

Border Rep

4 3 2 1
6 sts

Foundation

2 1
6 sts

PAT 3
Border, Transition, and Main Pat rep

2 ∩ 1
3 sts

Foundation

2 1
3 sts

PAT 2A
Border, Transition, and Main Pat rep

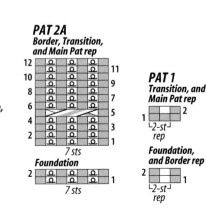

12 11 10 9 8 7 6 5 4 3 2 1
7 sts

Foundation

2 1
7 sts

PAT 1
Transition, and Main Pat rep

1 2
⌐2-st⌐ rep

Foundation, and Border rep

2 1
⌐2-st⌐ rep

Shape armholes

Bind off 5 (6, 6, 6) sts at beginning of next 2 rows, 4 (5, 5, 5) sts at beginning of next 2 rows, 3 (4, 4, 4) sts at beginning of next 2 rows, 2 (3, 3, 3) sts at beginning of next 2 rows. Dec 1 st each side on next row, then every other row 9 (9, 10, 10) times more—146 (150, 158, 170) sts. Work even until armhole measures 9¼ (9¼, 9½, 9½)", end with row 13 (13, 5, 5) of Pats 5A and 5B.

Shape neck

Next row (WS) Work 49 (51, 54, 60) sts in pat, join 2nd ball of yarn and bind off center 48 (48, 50, 50) sts, work to end. Working both sides at same time, bind off from each neck edge 12 (12, 13, 13) sts once. *Next row* (RS) Work cable nearest right neck edge as 2/2 RPC, and cable nearest left neck edge as 2/2 LPC. Work 1 row even. Place rem 37 (39, 41, 47) sts each side on hold.

Right Front

With size 2.25mm (US 1) needles, cast on 86 (92, 97, 103) sts. *Begin Chart pats: Foundation row 1* (RS) Work 16 sts Pat 7 Right Front, p0 (0, 1, 1) (rev St st), 8 sts Pat 6B, p0 (0, 1, 1) (rev St st), 18 sts Pat 5B, p0 (0, 1, 1) (rev St st), 7 sts Pat 2B, 3 sts Pat 3, p0 (1, 1, 1) (rev St st), 6 sts Pat 4B, p0 (1, 1, 1) (rev St st), 3 sts Pat 3, 7 sts Pat 2B, 17 (21, 23, 29) sts Pat 1, k1 (selvage st). *Row 2* Work Foundation row 2 in established pat. Work Border Rep Chart for all pats for 27 (27, 31, 31) rows more. Change to size 2.75mm (US 2) needles. *Next row* (WS) Continue Pats 2B, 3, 6B and 7 as set; work row 1 of Transition for Pats 1, 4B and 5B. *Next row* (RS) Work row 1 of Transition Chart for Pat 7 Right Front, working all other pats as set. Work through row 5 of Transition Chart for Pat 4B. *Next row* (RS) Begin Main Pat rep for Pat 4B. Work 1 row even. *Next row* (RS) Begin Main Pat rep for Pat 5B. Work through row 10 of Transition Chart for Pat 7 Right Front. Change to size 3.25mm (US 3) needles. *Next row* (RS) Begin Main Pat rep for Pat 7 Right Front—94 (100, 105, 111) sts. Continue in pat as established through 3 reps of Main Pat rep Chart for Pat 7. Piece measures approximately 9 (9, 9¼, 9¼)" from beginning.

Shape neck and armhole

Begin Pat 7 Right Front Neck Dec Chart, maintaining other pats, AT SAME TIME, when piece measures same length as back to underarm, shape armhole at begin-ning of WS rows as for back. After completing row 14 of Neck Dec Chart, continue to dec 1 st at neck edge on WS rows through remaining sts of Pat 7, then across sts of Pat 6B (working ssp over center 6 sts, and keeping garter st selvage at neck edge), until 2 (4, 4, 4) sts of Chart 6B, plus 1 selvage st remain.

Sizes S, M only Work next WS row without a dec, then work dec on next WS row.
Sizes L, 1X only Work a p3tog tbl on next WS row, then resume single decs every WS row twice more.

All Sizes Continue with Pat 5B Right Front Neck dec Chart, rep rows 27–42, end with row 44 (44, 52, 52). Place rem 37 (39, 41, 47) sts on hold.

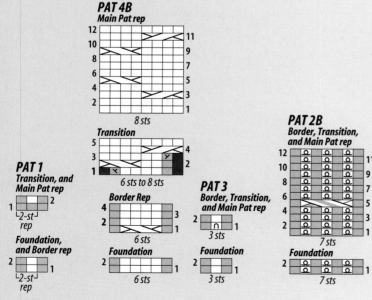

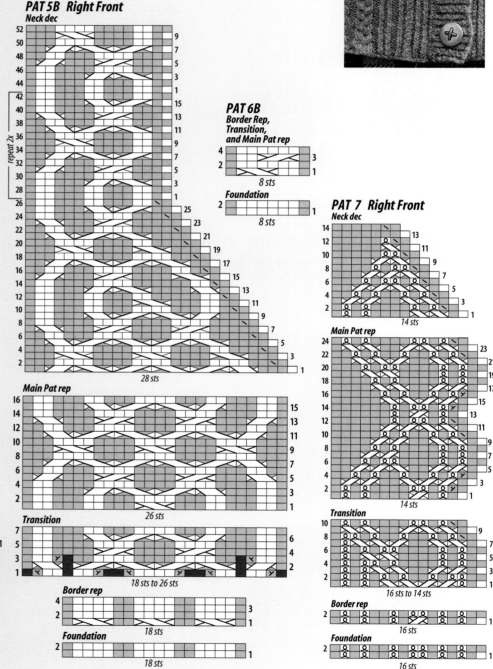

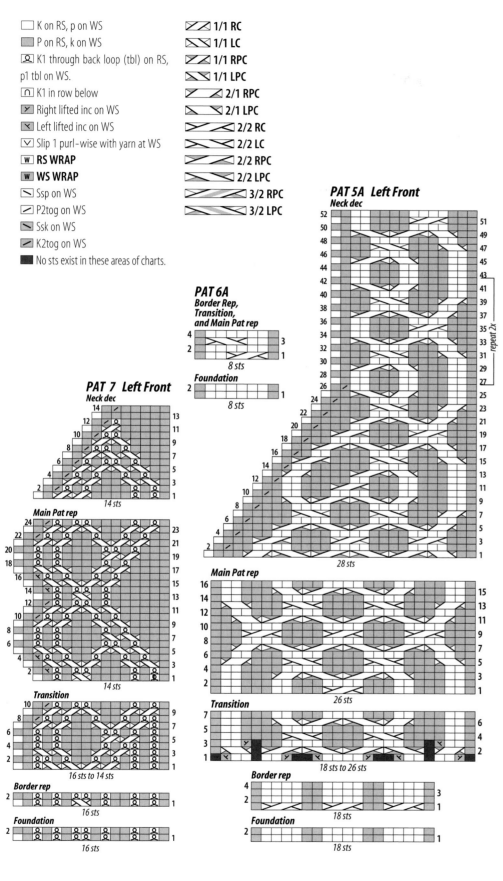

K on RS, p on WS
P on RS, k on WS
K1 through back loop (tbl) on RS, p1 tbl on WS.
K1 in row below
Right lifted inc on WS
Left lifted inc on WS
Slip 1 purl-wise with yarn at WS
W RS WRAP
W WS WRAP
Ssp on WS
P2tog on WS
Ssk on WS
K2tog on WS
No sts exist in these areas of charts.

1/1 RC
1/1 LC
1/1 RPC
1/1 LPC
2/1 RPC
2/1 LPC
2/2 RC
2/2 LC
2/2 RPC
2/2 LPC
3/2 RPC
3/2 LPC

PAT 5A   Left Front
Neck dec
28 sts
repeat 2x

PAT 6A
Border Rep, Transition, and Main Pat rep
8 sts
Foundation
8 sts

PAT 7   Left Front
Neck dec
14 sts
Main Pat rep
14 sts
Transition
16 sts to 14 sts
Border rep
16 sts
Foundation
16 sts

Main Pat rep
26 sts
Transition
18 sts to 26 sts
Border rep
18 sts
Foundation
18 sts

Left Front

With size 2.25mm (US 1) needles, cast on 86 (92, 97, 103) sts. *Foundation row 1* (RS) K1 (salvage st), work 17 (21, 23, 29) sts Pat 1, 7 sts Pat 2A, 3 sts Pat 3, p0 (1, 1, 1) (rev St st), 6 sts Pat 4A, p0 (1, 1, 1) (rev St st), 3 sts Pat 3, 7 sts Pat 2A, p0 (0, 1, 1) (rev St st), 18 sts Pat 5A, p0 (0, 1, 1) (rev St st), 8 sts Pat 6A, p0 (0, 1, 1) (rev St st), work 16 sts Pat 7 Left Front. Continue as for right front, reversing armhole and neck shaping (work k2tog in place of ssk, and p2tog or p3tog in place of ssp or p3tog tbl).

Armbands *MAKE 2*

With circular needle, cast on 258 (265, 279, 286) sts. Work 2 rows of Band Chart 5 times. Do not bind off. Place sts on hold.

Front and neckband

Place markers for 8 buttonholes along right front edge, with the first ½" from lower edge, the last ½" below neck dec, and 6 others spaced evenly between, centered in zigzags. With circular needle, cast on 587 (587, 607, 607) sts. *Begin Band Chart: Row 1* (RS) K1 (salvage st), work first 3 sts of chart 1 (1, 2, 2) times, work 7-st rep across to last 9 (9, 12, 12) sts, work last 8 sts of chart once, then work last 3 sts 0 (0, 1, 1) time more, k1 (salvage st). Continue in pat as established until 5 rows have been worked. *Row 6* (WS) Work in pat, binding off 6 sts to correspond to each buttonhole marker. On next row, cast on 6 sts over each set of bound-off sts. Work 1 row even. *Next row* (RS) Work 32 (32, 35, 35) sts in pat, work 6 reps of Short Row Chart, work to last 114 (114, 117, 117) sts. Work 6 reps of Short Row Chart, work in pat to end. Work 1 row even. Do not bind off.

Finishing

Join shoulders, using 3-needle bind-off. Sew open sts of bands, matching short-row triangles of front band to zigzags of front edge. Block. Sew side seams. Sew on buttons.

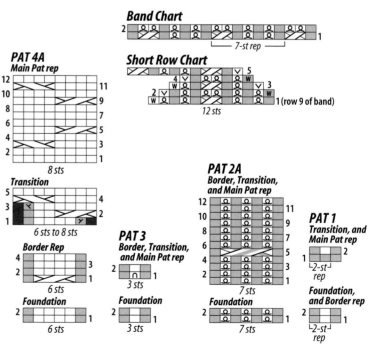

Band Chart
7-st rep

Short Row Chart
12 sts
1 (row 9 of band)

PAT 4A
Main Pat rep
8 sts
Transition
6 sts to 8 sts
Border Rep
6 sts
Foundation
6 sts

PAT 3
Border, Transition, and Main Pat rep
3 sts
Foundation
3 sts

PAT 2A
Border, Transition, and Main Pat rep
7 sts
Foundation
7 sts

PAT 1
Transition, and Main Pat rep
2-st rep
Foundation, and Border rep
2-st rep

This garment combines multiple, highly textured stitch patterns randomly and without gauge problems. It is a challenge but also, I think, a wonderful learning experience. Choose a smooth yarn to show off the textures; mercerized cotton is especially effective.

Sally Melville

A vest of many stitches

Notes

1 See *School*, p. 102, for Make 1 (M1K and M1P), ssk, SK2P, and p2tog. **2** At times, incs or decs within pats result in 'no stitch' symbols that maintain the chart's integrity. Simply skip the symbol and work the next st. **3** Selvage stitches are not included on charts nor on written instructions (except where indicated). Work selvage stitches in St st. **4** Unless otherwise indicated, sl sts purlwise. **5** Jogs at side edges of charts do not always represent shaping; they may reflect incs or decs within pats. For best results, read through shaping directions in written pat. **6** See charts on pp. 68–73.

Back

With smaller needles, cast on 119 (131, 143, 155) sts. Beginning and ending with k1, work 7 rows in k1, p1 rib. Change to larger needles.

For size S only: Next row (WS) P1 (selvage st), p30, [p into front and back of next st, p8] 4 times, p51, p1 (selvage)—123 sts.

For sizes M, L, 1X: P 1 row on WS.

For all sizes: (See Note 3 above and Back chart, pp. 68–69) Beginning with chart row 25 (19, 11, 1) and work to row 96 (92, 88, 84) of chart for Back. Piece measures approx 9 (9½, 10, 10½)" from beginning—122 (134, 146, 158) sts.

Shape armholes

Bind off 12 sts at beginning of next 2 rows. Dec 1 st each side (working ssk after first selvage st and k2tog before last selvage st) every other row 7 (9, 10, 12) times—85 (93, 103, 111) sts. When piece measures 18½ (19½, 20½, 21½)" from beginning, end with chart row 176—84 (92, 102, 110) sts.

Shape neck and shoulders

Row 177 Work 28 (31, 34, 37) sts in pat, place next 33 (35, 39, 41) sts on hold, join 2nd ball of yarn and work rem 23 (26, 29, 32) sts in pat. At each neck edge, dec 1 st 3 times, AT SAME TIME and beginning on row 179, bind off from each shoulder (including selvages) 5 (6, 7, 7) sts twice, 5 (6, 7, 8) sts once, 6 (6, 6, 8) sts once.

Skill Experienced
Fit Standard
Sizes S (M, L, 1X). Shown in Small.
Finished measurements 38 (42, 46, 50)" around, when buttoned, and 19½ (20½, 21½, 22½)" long.
Gauge 23 sts and 30 rows to 10cm/4" in St st, using larger needles.
24 sts and 36 rows to 10cm/4" over pattern sts using larger needles.
Yarn 950 (1100, 1270, 1450) yds. Light weight.
Needles Size 3.25 and 3.75mm/US 3 and 5, *or size to obtain gauge.*
Buttons Five 20mm/¾".
Extras Cable needle (cn). Stitch markers.
Original yarn Cascade/Austermann Smaragd (100% wool, 1¾oz/50g, 136yds/125m).

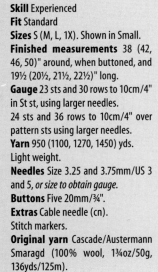

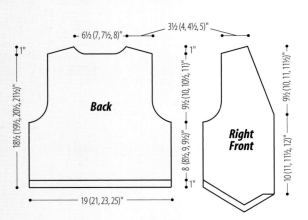

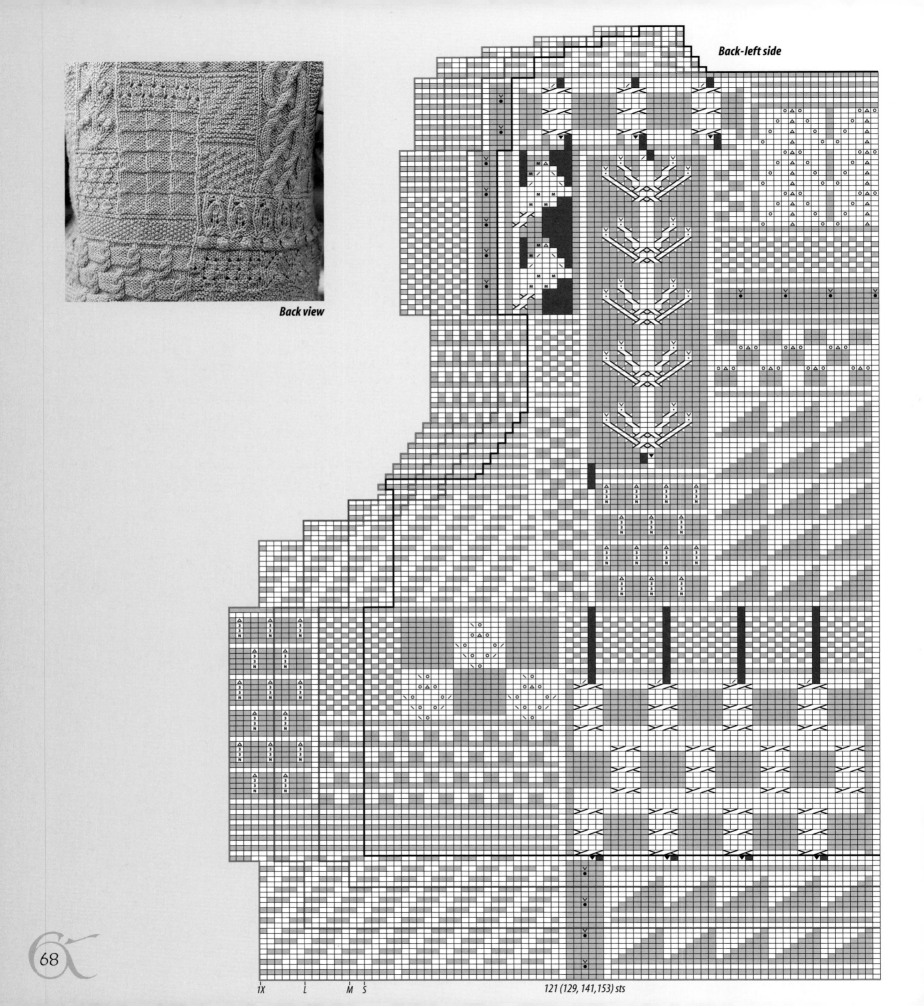

Back view

121 (129, 141, 153) sts

1X   L   M S

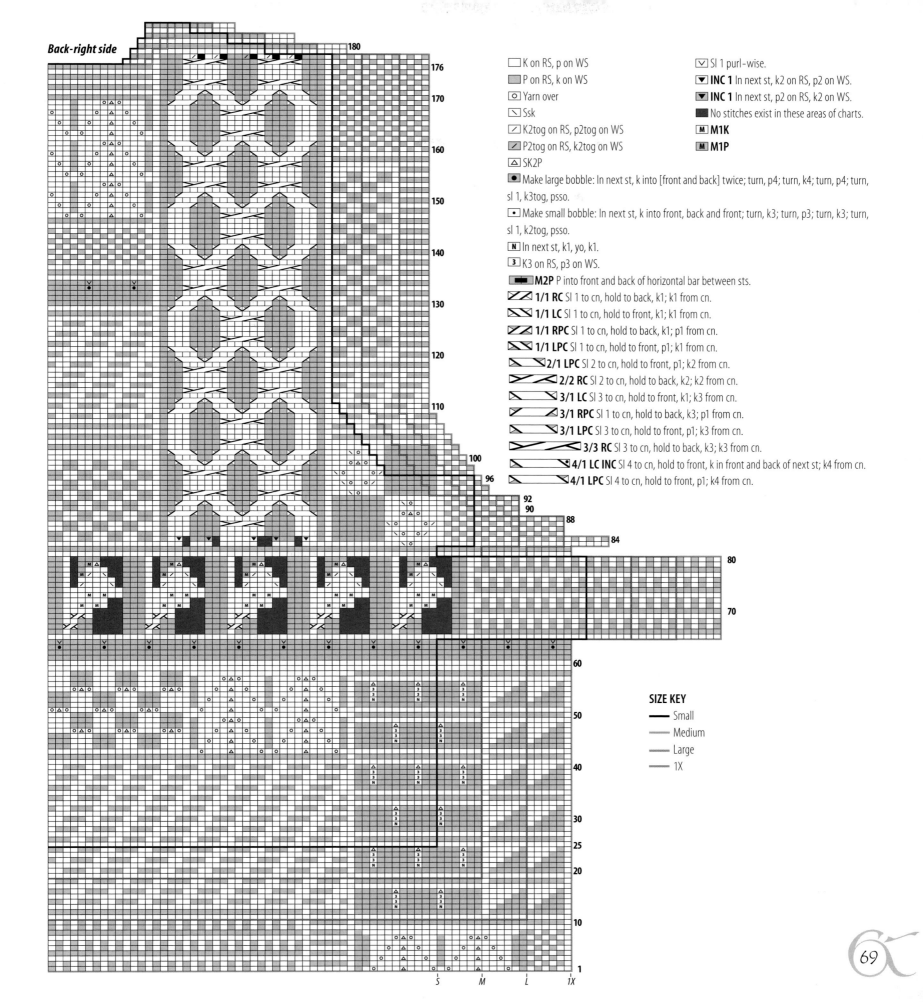

Back-right side

180
176
170
160
150
140
130
120
110
100
96
92
90
88
84
80
70
60
50
40
30
25
20
10
1

□ K on RS, p on WS

▨ P on RS, k on WS

◉ Yarn over

◫ Ssk

◩ K2tog on RS, p2tog on WS

◪ P2tog on RS, k2tog on WS

△ SK2P

● Make large bobble: In next st, k into [front and back] twice; turn, p4; turn, k4; turn, p4; turn, sl 1, k3tog, psso.

• Make small bobble: In next st, k into front, back and front; turn, k3; turn, p3; turn, k3; turn, sl 1, k2tog, psso.

N In next st, k1, yo, k1.

3 K3 on RS, p3 on WS.

◄► M2P P into front and back of horizontal bar between sts.

▨ 1/1 RC Sl 1 to cn, hold to back, k1; k1 from cn.

▨ 1/1 LC Sl 1 to cn, hold to front, k1; k1 from cn.

▨ 1/1 RPC Sl 1 to cn, hold to back, k1; p1 from cn.

▨ 1/1 LPC Sl 1 to cn, hold to front, p1; k1 from cn.

▨ 2/1 LPC Sl 2 to cn, hold to front, p1; k2 from cn.

▨ 2/2 RC Sl 2 to cn, hold to back, k2; k2 from cn.

▨ 3/1 LC Sl 3 to cn, hold to front, k1; k3 from cn.

▨ 3/1 RPC Sl 1 to cn, hold to back, k3; p1 from cn.

▨ 3/1 LPC Sl 3 to cn, hold to front, p1; k3 from cn.

▨ 3/3 RC Sl 3 to cn, hold to back, k3; k3 from cn.

▨ 4/1 LC INC Sl 4 to cn, hold to front, k in front and back of next st; k4 from cn.

▨ 4/1 LPC Sl 4 to cn, hold to front, p1; k4 from cn.

☑ Sl 1 purl-wise.

▼ INC 1 In next st, k2 on RS, p2 on WS.

▼ INC 1 In next st, p2 on RS, k2 on WS.

■ No stitches exist in these areas of charts.

M M1K

M M1P

SIZE KEY

— Small

— Medium

— Large

— 1X

S M L 1X

Right Front

With smaller needles, cast on 87 (96, 105, 111) sts. **Row 1** Beginning with k1, work k1, p1 rib over 42 sts, k1, place marker (pm), k1, pm, beginning with k1, work k1, p1 rib over 42 (50, 60, 66) sts, k1 (2, 1, 1). **Row 2** P1, inc 1 in next st, rib to 2 sts before marker, k2tog, p1, ssk, rib to last 2 sts, inc 1 in next st, p1. **Row 3** K1, rib across, end k2 (1, 2, 2). **Row 4** P1, inc 1 in next st, rib to 2 sts before marker, p2tog, p1, p2tog through back loop (tbl), rib to last 2 sts, inc 1 in next st, p1. Rep rows 1–3 once more (sl markers). Change to larger needles and rep row 4. Cut yarn. **Begin chart and short rows: Row 1** With RS facing, sl to marked st, remove marker, k1, turn, p1, *p2tog, p1, turn, sl 1, work next row of chart, ssk, k1, turn, sl 1, work next row of chart, p2tog tbl, p1, turn, sl 1, work next row of chart, k2tog, k1, turn, sl 1, work chart; rep from* through chart row 27. **Next row** Sl 1, work chart row 28, p2tog tbl, p2, turn.

For size S only: Next row K1 selvage, work from chart to 4 sts rem at side edge, k2tog, k2.

For sizes M, L, 1X: Continue to work from chart and work selvage st at center front edge to 4 (4, 10) sts rem at side edge—row 35 (41, 41).

For size M only: Work those sts as ssk, k2.

For sizes L, 1X only: Work those sts as k2tog, k2 (8).

For all sizes: Continue in chart pat, (see Note 3, p. 66) AT SAME TIME and beginning on row 102 (110, 118, 126), shape armhole as for back at beginning of WS rows and shape neck at beginning of RS rows (beginning on row 111 (119, 123, 131). Shape neck by dec 1 st at neck edge every 4th row 19 (20, 22, 23) times. When armhole measures same as back to shoulder, shape shoulder as for back.

Key

☐ K on RS, p on WS
▨ P on RS, k on WS
○ Yarn over
╱ Ssk
▨ K2tog on RS, p2tog on WS
▨ P2tog on RS, k2tog on WS
△ SK2P
● **Make large bobble:** In next st, k into [front and back] twice; turn, p4; turn, k4; turn, p4; turn, sl 1, k3tog, psso.
• **Make small bobble:** In next st, k into front, back and front; turn, k3; turn, p3; turn, k3; turn, sl 1, k2tog, psso.
N In next st, k1, yo, k1.
3 K3 on RS, p3 on WS.

☑ Sl 1 purl-wise.
► **INC 1** In next st, k2 on RS, p2 on WS.
► **INC 1** In next st, p2 on RS, k2 on WS.
■ No stitches exist in these areas of charts.
M **M1K**
M **M1P**

■ **M2P** P into front and back of horizontal bar between sts.
◿ **1/1 RC** Sl 1 to cn, hold to back, k1; k1 from cn.
◿ **1/1 LC** Sl 1 to cn, hold to front, k1; k1 from cn.
◿ **1/1 RPC** Sl 1 to cn, hold to back, k1; p1 from cn.
◿ **1/1 LPC** Sl 1 to cn, hold to front, p1; k1 from cn.
◿ **2/1 LPC** Sl 2 to cn, hold to front, p1; k2 from cn.
◿ **2/2 RC** Sl 2 to cn, hold to back, k2; k2 from cn.
◿ **3/1 LC** Sl 3 to cn, hold to front, k1; k3 from cn.
◿ **3/1 RPC** Sl 1 to cn, hold to back, k3; p1 from cn.
◿ **3/1 LPC** Sl 3 to cn, hold to front, p1; k3 from cn.
◿ **3/3 RC** Sl 3 to cn, hold to back, k3; k3 from cn.
◿ **4/1 LC INC** Sl 4 to cn, hold to front, k in front and back of next st, k4 from cn.
◿ **4/1 LPC** Sl 4 to cn, hold to front, p1; k4 from cn.

SIZE KEY

— Small
— Medium
— Large
— 1X

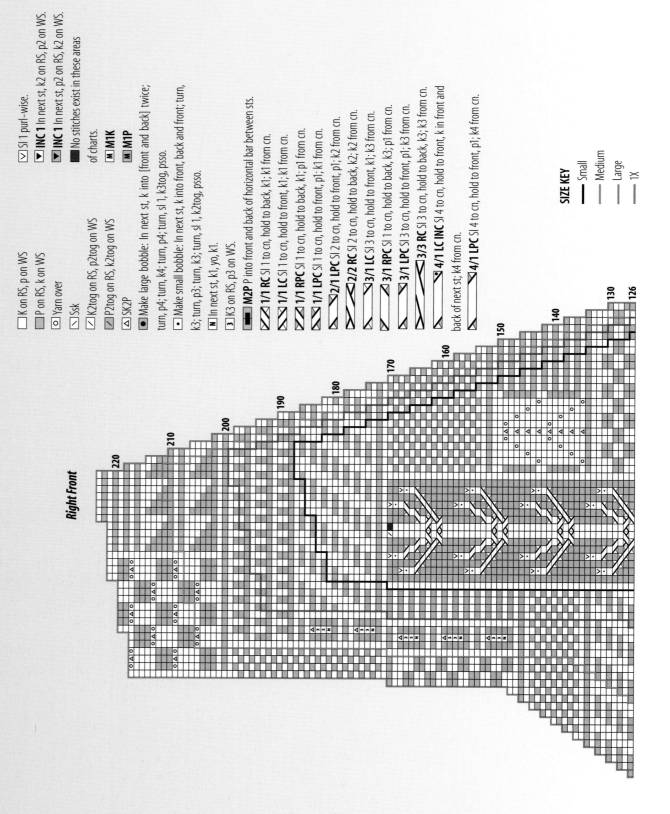

Right Front

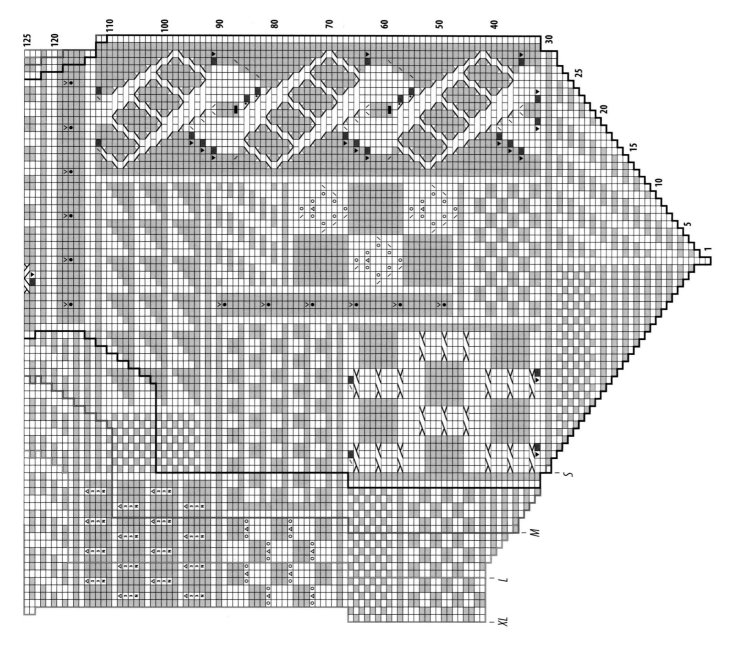

Left Front

With smaller needles, cast on 87 (96, 105, 111) sts. **Row 1** K0 (1, 0, 0), beginning with k1, work in k1, p1 rib over 42 (50, 60, 66) sts, k1, pm, k1, work in k1, p1 rib over 42 sts, end k1. **Row 2** P1, inc 1 in next st, rib to 2 sts before marker, k2tog, p1, ssk, rib to last 2 sts, inc 1 in next st, p1. **Row 3** K2 (1, 2, 2), rib across, end k1. **Row 4** P1, inc 1 in next st, rib to 2 sts before marker, p2tog, p1, p2tog tbl, rib to last 2 sts, inc 1 in next st, p1. Rep rows 1-3 once more. Change to larger needles and rep row 4. Cut yarn. **Begin chart and short rows: Row 1** Work as for right front through row 27.

For size S only: Next row Sl 1, work to 4 sts rem at side edge, p2tog tbl, p2.

Next row K1 selvage, work chart to 4 sts rem at center front edge, k2tog, k2.

For sizes M, L, 1X: Work next WS row as established, turn, sl 1, work chart to 4 sts rem at center front edge, k2 tog, k2. Continue to work from chart as established and work selvage st at center front edge. **Row 34 (40, 40), for size M only:** Work 4 sts rem at side edge by p2tog, p2; **for sizes L, 1X,** work 4 (10) sts rem at side edge by p2tog tbl, p2 (8).

For all sizes: Continue chart pat (see Note 3, p. 66) until piece measures same as back to underarm along straight edge. Reverse armhole, neck and shoulder shaping to correspond to right front.

Key

☐ K on RS, p on WS
▨ P on RS, k on WS
○ Yarn over
⟋ Ssk
⟍ K2tog on RS, p2tog on WS
⟋ P2tog on RS, k2tog on WS
◺ SK2P
● Make large bobble: In next st, k into [front and back] twice; turn, p4; turn, k4; turn, p4; turn, sl 1, k3tog, psso.
• Make small bobble: In next st, k into front, back and front; turn, k3; turn, p3; turn, k3; turn, sl 1, k2tog, psso.
Ⓝ In next st, k1, yo, k1.
3 K3 on RS, p3 on WS.
▽ Sl 1 purl-wise.
▶ INC 1 In next st, k2 on RS, p2 on WS.
▼ INC 1 In next st, p2 on RS, k2 on WS.
■ No stitches exist in these areas of charts.
Ⓜ M1K
Ⓜ M1P
▬ M2P P into front and back of horizontal bar between sts.
⟋ 1/1 RC Sl 1 to cn, hold to back, k1; k1 from cn.
⟍ 1/1 LC Sl 1 to cn, hold to front, k1; k1 from cn.
⟋ 1/1 RPC Sl 1 to cn, hold to back, k1; p1 from cn.
⟍ 1/1 LPC Sl 1 to cn, hold to front, p1; k1 from cn.
⟋ 2/1 LPC Sl 2 to cn, hold to front, p1; k2 from cn.
⟍ 2/2 RC Sl 2 to cn, hold to back, k2; k2 from cn.
⟋ 3/1 LC Sl 3 to cn, hold to front, k1; k3 from cn.
⟍ 3/1 RPC Sl 1 to cn, hold to back, k3; p1 from cn.
⟋ 3/1 LPC Sl 3 to cn, hold to front, p1; k3 from cn.
⟍ 3/3 RC Sl 3 to cn, hold to back, k3; k3 from cn.
⟋ 4/1 LC INC Sl 4 to cn, hold to front, k in front and back of next st; k4 from cn.
⟍ 4/1 LPC Sl 4 to cn, hold to front, p1; k4 from cn.

SIZE KEY
── Small
── Medium
── Large
── 1X

Left Front

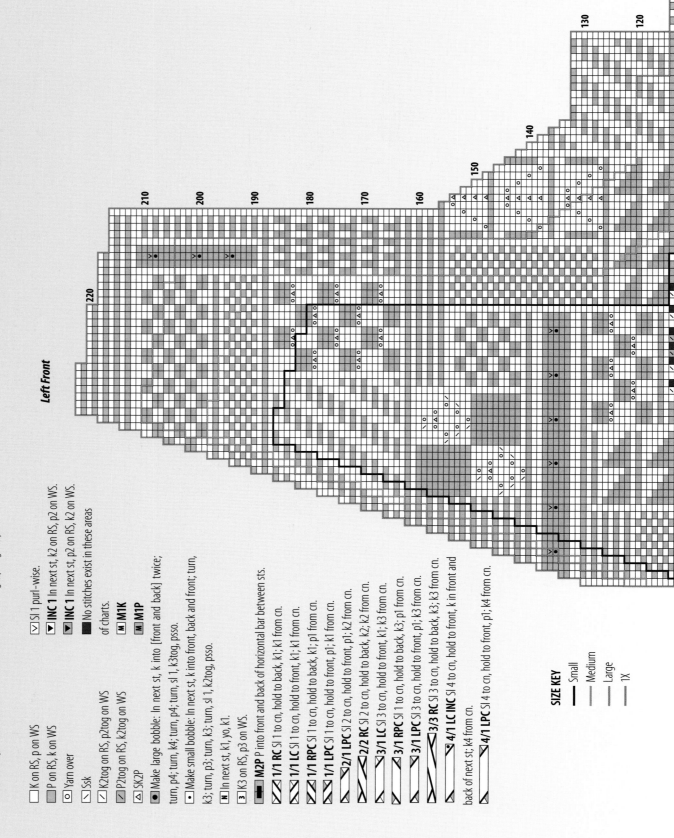

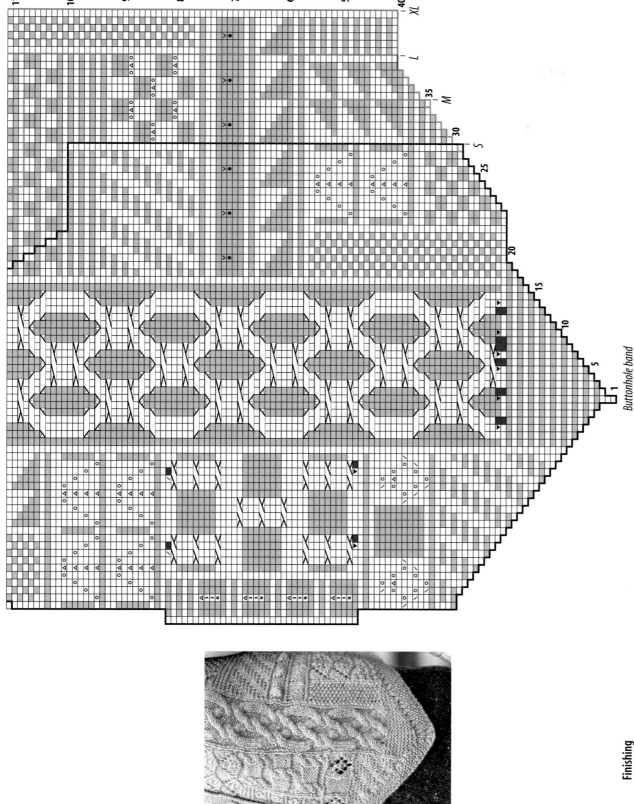

Finishing

Block pieces. Sew shoulder seams. Work all bands as follows: Use smaller needles and begin with RS facing.

Armhole bands

Pick up and k12 sts at underarm, 60 (69, 78, 87) sts to shoulder seam (approx 3 sts to 4 rows), 61 (70, 79, 88) sts to underarm, 12 sts at underarm. *Next row* (WS) Beginning with p1, work k1, p1 rib across. Rib 6 rows more. Bind off all sts. Sew side seams, including bands.

Buttonband

Beginning at center back neck, pick up and k17 (18, 20, 21) along neck, 9 sts along back neck shaping, 67 (70, 77, 80) sts from shoulder to beginning of neck shaping (approx 7 sts to 8 rows), 3 sts at point of V-neck, 75 (81, 84, 90) sts to lower edge (approx 5 sts to 6 rows). Work 7 rows in k1, p1 rib as for armholes.

Buttonhole band

Beginning at lower right front edge and pick up 75 (81, 84, 90) sts to beginning of V-neck shaping, 3 sts at point of V-neck, 67 (70, 77, 80) sts to shoulder, 9 sts along back neck shaping, 17 (18, 20, 21) sts at back neck. *Row 1* (WS) Beginning with p1, work in k1, p1 rib. *Row 2* Rib 6 sts, ssk, yo twice (buttonhole), *rib 14 (16, 16, 18) sts, ssk, yo twice, rep from* 3 times, rib to end. *Row 3* *Rib to double yo, drop first yo and k 2nd yo tbl; rep from*; rib to end. *Row 4* *Rib to buttonhole, p1 through hole, drop p st formed from working through yo, rep from* to last buttonhole, rib to end. *Rows 5–7* Work in k1, p1 rib. Bind off all sts. Sew bands tog at back neck. Sew on buttons. ∩

family Arans

To my mind a classic represents the best of old and new. These pullovers are inspired by the distinctive style and design simplicity of Scottish fisherman ganseys. Reminiscent of those telltale samplers with brocade-like stitchwork, this design features all-over vertical textured patterns.

Kathy Zimmerman

Guernsey gals . . .

WOMAN'S/CHILD'S

Notes

1 See *School*, p. 102, for 3-needle bind-off. *2* Child sizes are given in parentheses; adult sizes follow in brackets. If there is only one figure or set of instructions, it applies to all sizes. For ease in working, circle the numbers for your size.

Back

With smaller needles, cast on (59, 73, 87) [95, 109, 123, 135] sts. *Begin rib pat: Next row* (WS) P1, *k1, p1; rep from* to end. Work 2 more rows in rib. K 3 rows. Work 5 rows in rib, inc (7, 8, 9) [11, 12, 13, 16] sts evenly across last row—(66, 81, 96) [106, 121, 136, 151] sts. Change to larger needles. P 1 row. K 1 row. *Begin Body/Sleeve Chart:* Beginning and ending as indicated for body, work until piece measures (8, 8½, 9) [12½, 13, 13½, 14]" from beginning, end with a WS row. P 1 row. K 1 row, dec (9, 8, 15) [17, 16, 15, 22] sts evenly across—(57, 73, 81) [89, 105, 121, 129] sts. *Begin Chart C: Next row* (RS) Work 8-st rep of Chart C to last st, work last st of chart. Continue in pat as established through chart row 8. K 2 rows. Piece measures (10, 10½, 11) [14½, 15, 15½, 16]" from beginning.

Shape armhole

P 2 rows, binding off (4) [6, 8, 10, 10] sts at beginning of each row—(49, 65, 73) [77, 89, 101, 109] sts.

Yoke

Begin Yoke chart: Beginning and ending as indicated, work chart until armhole measures (5, 5½, 6) [7½, 8, 8½, 9]", end with a WS row.

Shape neck

Next row (RS) Continue pats, work (13, 20, 23) [24, 28, 32, 35] sts, place center (23, 25, 27) [29, 33, 37, 39] sts on hold, join 2nd ball of yarn and work to end. Working both sides at same time, dec 1 st at each neck edge every other row twice—(11, 18, 21) [22, 26, 30, 33] sts each side. Work even until armhole measures (6, 6½, 7) [8½, 9, 9½, 10]". Place sts on hold.

Front

Work as for back until armhole measures (3½, 4, 4½) [6, 6½, 7, 7½]", end with a WS row.

Shape neck

Next row (RS) Work (15, 22, 25) [26, 30, 34, 37] sts, place center (19, 21, 23) [25, 29, 33, 35] sts on hold, join 2nd ball of yarn and work to end. Working both sides at same time, dec 1 st at each neck edge every other row 4 times. Work even until

armhole measures same as back to shoulders. Place rem (11, 18, 21) [22, 26, 30, 33] sts on hold.

Sleeves

With smaller needles, cast on (33, 33, 37) [51, 55, 57, 59] sts. Work rib as for back, inc (7, 7, 5) [4, 6, 4, 4] sts evenly across last row—(40, 40, 42) [55, 61, 61, 63] sts. Change to larger needles. P 1 row. K 1 row. *Begin Body/Sleeve Chart:* Beginning and ending as indicated for sleeve, work chart pat, AT SAME TIME, inc 1 st each side (working incs into pat) on 5th row, then every 4th row (7, 13, 15) [11, 5, 15, 16] times more, every 6th row (7, 4, 4) [10, 15, 9, 9] times—(70, 76, 82) [99, 103, 111, 115] sts. Work even until piece measures (13, 14, 15) [18¼, 19½, 20½, 21]" from beginning, end with a WS row. P 1 row. K 1 row. Bind off all sts.

Finishing

Block pieces. Join shoulders tog, using 3-needle bind-off.

Neckband

With RS facing and circular needle, begin at left shoulder seam, pick up and k (78, 80, 82) [92, 96, 100, 104] sts evenly around neck edge, including sts from holders. Place marker, join and work in rnds as follows: P 2 rnds, work 5 rnds k1, p1 rib. K 1 rnd, p 1 rnd, k 1 rnd. Work 3 rnds k1, p1 rib. Bind off all sts in rib. Set in sleeves. Sew side and sleeve seams.

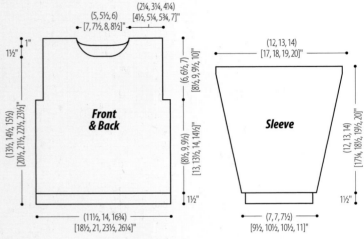

BOTH

Skill Intermediate

Fit Loose

CHILD'S

Sizes 1/2 (4/6, 8/10). Shown in 4/6.

Finished measurements 23 (28, 33½)" around and 16 (17, 18)" long.

Yarn 700 (855, 1050) yds. Medium weight.

WOMAN'S

Sizes XS/S (M, L, 1X). Shown in Medium.

Finished measurements 37 (42, 47, 52½)" around and 23 (24, 25, 26)" long.

Yarn 1375 (1610, 1830, 2075) yds. Medium weight.

BOTH

Gauge 23 sts and 27 rows to 10cm/4" over Charts A and B, using larger needles.

Needles Size 4 and 5mm/US 6 and 8, *or size to obtain gauge.*

Size 4mm/US 6 circular, 40cm/16" long.

Extras Cable needle (cn).

Stitch markers and holders.

Original yarn *Child's:* Lion Brand Al-pa-ka (40% acrylic, 30% alpaca, 30% wool; 1¾oz/50g, 107 yds/96m). *Woman's:* Plymouth Galway (100% wool, 3½oz/100g, 230 yds/207m).

Chart for Body/Sleeve

6

4
2

15-st repeat

5

3
1

Body (Child's)
Sleeve 1/2, 4/6, XS/S
Sleeve 8/10
Body (Adult's); Sleeve M, L
Sleeve 1X

Body (Child's)
Sleeve 1/2, 4/6, XS/S
Sleeve 8/10
Body (Adult's); Sleeve M, L
Sleeve 1X

Chart C

8
6
4
2

7
5
3
1

8-st rep

☐ K on RS, p on WS.
▨ P on RS, k on WS.
� **2/2 RC** Sl 2
to cn, hold to back, k2; k2
from cn.

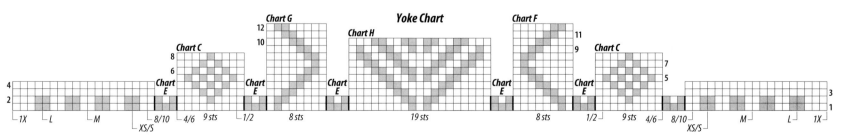

Chart G

12
10

Chart C

8
6

4
2

Chart E

Yoke Chart

Chart H

Chart E

Chart F

11
9

Chart C

Chart E

7
5

3
1

1X   L   M

XS/S

8/10   4/6   9 sts   1/2   8 sts   19 sts   8 sts   1/2   9 sts   4/6   8/10   M   L   1X

XS/S

A fisherman knit sweater doesn't have to be a complicated arrangement of cables, bobbles, and other such stitch assortments. The Guernsey sweater is the simplest and most practical of the fisherman knits, using knit and purl combinations to form the patterns. This style of sweater has a few unique characteristics, including a decorative rib, side vents, yoke patterns, and gussets at the neck and underarm for ease.

It was fun to make two 'father and son' pullovers, but they'd work equally well for a mother and daughter. Kids look great in oversized, grown-up sweaters, especially fisherman knits. This pattern is a perfect introduction for someone who is intimidated by cables and patternwork.

Penny Olman

. . . and guys

MAN'S/CHILD'S

Note

Child sizes are given in parentheses; adult sizes follow in brackets. If there is only one figure or set of instructions, it applies to all sizes. For ease in working, circle the numbers for your size.

Garter rib pat *ANY NUMBER OF STS*

Row 1 (RS) Purl. *Rows 2 and 3* Knit. *Row 4* Purl. Rep rows 1–4 for Garter rib pat.

Back

With larger needles, cast on (77, 85, 95) [105, 115, 127, 133] sts. Work (20) [28] rows in Garter rib pat. *Begin Dotted pat chart:* Beginning and ending as indicated for body, work chart pat until piece measures (10½, 11, 11½) [15, 15½, 16, 16]" from beginning, end with a WS row.
Yoke

Work 4 rows of Garter rib pat, then work rows 1 and 2 once more. *Begin Yoke pat chart: Next row* (RS) Begin as indicated, work to center st, work center st, then work chart from left to right (do not work center st again), end at starting point. Continue in pat as established until piece measures (17½, 18½, 19½) [24½, 25½, 26½, 26½]" from beginning, end with a WS row.
Shape neck

Next row (RS) Continue pats, work (31, 35, 40) [42, 47, 53, 56] sts, join a 2nd ball of yarn and bind off center 15 [21] sts, work to end. Working both sides at same time, bind off from each neck edge (7, 8, 9) [5, 5, 6, 6] sts once, (0) [4, 5, 5, 6] sts once. Work even until piece measures (18, 19, 20) [25½, 26½, 27½, 27½]" from beginning. Bind off rem (24, 27, 31) [33, 37, 42, 44] sts each side.

Front

Work as for back until piece measures (15½, 16½, 17½) [22½, 23½, 24½, 24½]" from beginning, end with a WS row.
Shape neck

Next row (RS) Work (31, 35, 40) [45, 50, 55, 58] sts, join 2nd ball of yarn and bind off center (15) [15, 15, 17, 17] sts, work to end. Working both sides at same time, bind off from each neck edge (2) [3, 4, 4, 5] sts once, (2) [2, 3, 3, 3] sts once, (0) [2] sts (0) [1] time, then dec 1 st at each neck edge every other row (3, 4, 5) [5,

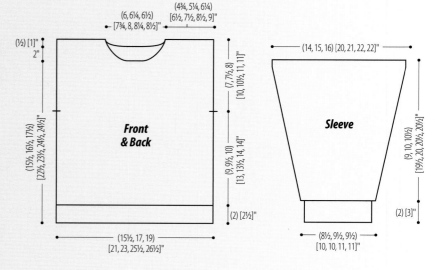

4, 4, 4] times. Work even until piece measures same as back to shoulders. Bind off rem (24, 27, 31) [33, 37, 42, 44] sts each side.

Sleeves

With smaller needles, cast on (38, 42, 42) [46, 46, 50, 50] sts. Work in k2, p2 rib for (2) [3]", inc 5 sts evenly across last row—(43, 47, 47) [51, 51, 55, 55] sts. *Begin Dotted pat chart:* Beginning and ending as for sleeve, work chart pat, AT SAME TIME, inc 1 st each side on 5th row, then every 4th row (13, 10, 14) [16, 14, 12, 12] times more, every 6th row (0, 3, 1) [7, 12, 14, 14] times—(71, 75, 79) [99, 105, 109, 109] sts. Work even until piece measures (10, 11, 11½)" [21½, 22, 22½, 22½]" from beginning, end with a WS row. Work 8 rows Garter rib pat. Bind off all sts.

Finishing

Block pieces. Sew right shoulder seam.

Neckband

With RS facing and smaller needles, beginning at left shoulder seam, pick up and k (70, 74, 78) [90, 94, 98, 98] sts evenly around neck edge. Work in k2, p2 rib for (2) [2½]". Bind off in rib. Sew rem shoulder seam, including neckband. Place markers (7, 7½, 8) [10, 10½ , 11, 11]" down from shoulder on front and back. Sew top of sleeves between markers. Leaving Garter rib pat open, sew side and sleeve seams. ∩

BOTH
Skill Intermediate
Fit Loose
CHILD'S
Sizes 4 (6, 8). Shown in 6.
Finished measurements 31 (34, 38)" around and 18 (19, 20)" long.
Yarn 790 (920, 1055)yds. Medium weight.
MAN'S
Sizes S (M, L, 1X). Shown in Medium.
Finished measurements 42 (46, 51, 53)" around and 25½ (26½, 27½, 27½)" long.
Yarn 1615 (1790, 2015, 2070)yds. Medium weight.
BOTH
Gauge 20 sts and 28 rows to 10cm/ 4" over Dotted pat, using size 4.5mm/ US 7 needles.
Needles Size 4 and 4.5mm/US 6 and 7 needles, *or size to obtain gauge.*
Extras Cable needle (cn).
Original yarn *Child's:* Patons Canadiana (100% Monsanto acrylic; 3½oz/100g, 228 yds/208m). *Man's:* Patons Classic Wool (100% wool, 3½oz/100g, 223 yds/204m)

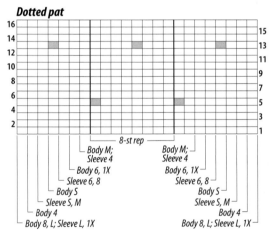

Dotted pat

8-st rep

Body M;
Sleeve 4
Body 6, 1X
Sleeve 6, 8
Body S
Sleeve S, M
Body 4
Body 8, L; Sleeve L, 1X

Body M;
Sleeve 4
Body 6, 1X
Sleeve 6, 8
Body S
Sleeve S, M
Body 4
Body 8, L; Sleeve L, 1X

Yoke pat

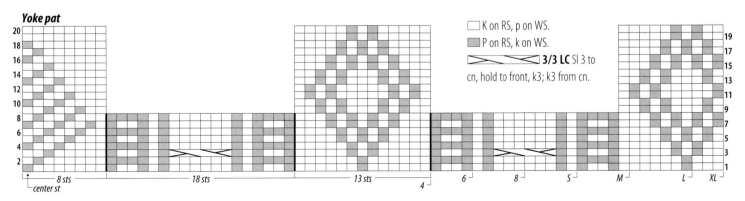

☐ K on RS, p on WS.

▨ P on RS, k on WS.

▨ **3/3 LC** Sl 3 to
cn, hold to front, k3; k3 from cn.

8 sts
center st
18 sts
13 sts
4
6
8
S
M
L
XL

An Aran Gansey is one of the most romantic and intricate creations of all the knitting traditions. Stories have been told, research undertaken, and books written that offer theories and facts about the development and symbolism of these textured wonders. Yet, whatever the age (or antiquity) of these designs, they are traditional and classic, fashionable and practical. You can be assured that you will never grow tired of knitting or wearing an Aran.

Nancy Bush

sailor's rib

Several traditions have come to be associated with the Aran Gansey; one is its shape: simple square lines, no armhole shaping, and a dropped shoulder. Another is the yarn: originally the natural white oily wool of Irish sheep, called Bainin (pronounced bawneen) was used. Today, Aran weight wools, which are slightly heavier than worsted weight, are available in a rainbow of colors. The lighter the color, the more the textures—all your hard work—will show up.

These designs can be knit circularly; however, it is more practical to work them flat. The reason lies within the cable patterns. The twists usually occur every so many rows (every 4th row for the OXO cable and every 6th row for the Rope cables). Working flat makes it easier to count these rows; you know that every right-side row is an even-or odd-numbered row, therefore only half the rows "count," and you'll be less likely to miss a cable turn when its row arrives.

In designing your own Aran, the first step is making swatches of patterns that appeal to you. Choose the yarn you plan to use for your garment, arm yourself with a selection of patterns from one of the many books available, and start knitting! Work up separate swatches of each pattern, bordered by several sts of garter or seed stitch to keep it from curling. Work at least 2 vertical repeats of the whole pattern to get a good idea of what it looks like. Keep notes on your swatches, where you found the pattern, how many stitches are needed, and what needle size you used.

The Sailor's Rib Gansey for children and adults is offered as a blank canvas. The pattern is given for those who wish to make it as it was originally designed, but it can also be changed, to allow you to create your own individual, unique gansey. Here is how. The center panel in the Sailor's Rib Gansey is the same in both the child's and the adult's pattern. It measures 6½" and contains 48 sts. With this in mind, choose from your knitted swatch collection several patterns that together equal close to 6½". You may have two favorite patterns, one for the center panel and one to place on each side of it, as I have done with the OXO and Rope cables; then add one or several tiny patterns, such as the 3-st Braid, to fill in. Or, you may want one larger pattern bordered on each side by a tiny one. Your swatches will help you plan. Play with your swatches, move them around, trying different ones next to each other to see how they look together. As you plan, try to choose patterns that vary in width; this will give more interest to the design. Use your imagination!

When you've selected the patterns you want, check to see how many stitches they require. If your stitch count in the center panel is more than 48 sts, your overall body width will be smaller than that given in the pattern. This is caused by the difference

in gauge between the center panel and the ribbed side panels. Note that the 48 sts in the center panel equal 6½" thus giving a stitch gauge of 7.3 sts per inch. The Sailor's Rib pattern at the sides has a gauge of 24 sts to 4" or 6 sts per inch. The cable panel draws in more. If you didn't change the number of sts in the original written pattern, yet used more in the center panel, deducting from the sides, your gansey would be slightly smaller. The opposite is also true. If you used fewer stitches in your center panel and worked more in the Sailor's Rib, your gansey would be larger.

If you add or subtract a few sts to maintain the size, divide them up evenly when you reach the neck shaping. For instance, if you've added 6 sts to the overall piece, place 2 in the left shoulder, 2 in the neck, and 2 in the right shoulder.

Making an Aran gansey is a rewarding experience, they work up more quickly than you would imagine—and they offer any knitter a challenge that is well worth the time spent.

Notes

1 See *School*, p. 102, for 3-needle bind-off. **2** First and last st of every row are worked in St st. **3** Chart D is the OXO cable, charts B and E are Rope cables, chart C is the 3-st Braid, charts A and F are Sailors Rib which is usually shown as a multiple of 5 sts plus 1 st, but have been broken up for convenience of this pattern. **4** Child's sizes are shown first followed by Men's sizes in brackets [].

Twisted Rib

Row 1 (RS) *P1, k1 through back loop (tbl); rep from *. *Row 2* *P1, k1; rep from *.

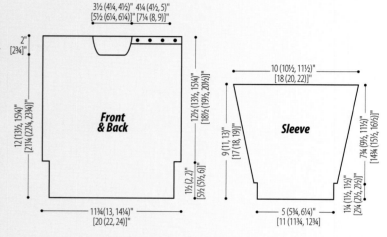

Skill Intermediate
Fit Standard
Sizes Child 2 (4, 6). Shown in 6. Men's [S (M, L)]. Shown in Large.
Finished measurements 23½ (26, 28½) [40 (44, 48)]" around and 14 (15½, 17¼) [24 (25, 26½)]" long.
Gauge 24 sts and 29 rows equal 10cm/4" over Chart A or F (Sailor's Rib pat), using larger needles.
Yarn 590 (740, 920) [1530 (1760, 2035)] yds. Medium weight.
Needles 3.25 and 4mm/US 3 and 6, or size to obtain gauge.
Buttons Child, five 12mm/½"; Men's five 15mm/⅝".
Extras Stitch holders. Cable needle (cn).
Original yarn Plymouth Aran 100 (100% wool; 3½oz/100g; 185 yds/168m).

Back

With smaller needles, cast on 66 (74, 84) [118 (124, 134)] sts. *Row 1* (RS) K1, work Twisted rib to last st, k1. Continue in pat as established until piece measures 1½ (2, 2) [5½ (5½, 6)]", ending with a RS row AND inc 8 (10, 10) [10 (16, 16)] sts evenly across that row—74 (84, 94) [128 (140, 150)] sts. Change to larger needles. *Next row* (WS) P1 (1, 1) [3 (1, 1)], [k1, p1] 1 (1, 1) [1 (0, 0)] times, [k1, p2, k1, p1] 2 (3, 4) [7 (9, 10)] times, k1, p1, k1, p6, k1, [p1, k1] twice, p3, k1, p1, k1, p8, k1, p1, k1, p3, k1, [p1, k1] twice, p6, k1, p1, k1, [p1, k1, p2, k1] 2 (3, 4) [7 (9, 10)]times, [p1, k1] 1 (1, 1) [1, 0, 0] times, p1 (1, 1) [3 (1, 1)]. *Begin Charts: Row 1* (RS) K1, begin where indicated, work 12 (17, 22) [39 (45, 50)] sts of Chart A, 3 sts Twisted rib, 6 sts chart B, 5 sts Twisted rib, 3 sts Chart C, 3 sts Twisted rib, 8 sts Chart D, 3 sts Twisted rib, 3 sts Chart C, 5 sts Twisted rib, 6 sts Chart E, 3 sts Twisted rib, 12 (17, 22) [39 (45, 50)] sts Chart F ending where indicated, k1. Continue in pats as established until piece measures 14 (15½, 17¼) [24 (25, 26½)]" from beginning, ending with a WS row. Place sts on hold.

Front

Work as for Back until piece measures 12 (13½, 15¼) [21¼ (22¼, 23¾)]" from beginning, ending with a WS row.

Shape neck

Note If a cable cross has to be omitted on one side of the neck, omit it on the other side.
Next Row (RS) Work 32 (36, 40) [56 (60, 65)] sts, place next 10(12, 14) [16 (20, 20)] sts on hold, join 2nd ball of yarn and work to end. Working both sides at same time, bind off at each neck edge 3 sts twice and 2 sts once (4 sts once and 3 sts twice; 4 sts once and 3 sts twice) [3 sts twice, 2 sts twice and 1 st twice (4 sts once, 3 sts once, 2 sts twice and 1 st twice; L same as M)]—24 (26, 30 [44 (47, 52)] sts each side. Work 1 row even. Place sts for left shoulder on hold. Continue on sts for right shoulder until piece is the same length as Back from beginning. Place sts on hold for buttonband.

Sleeves

With smaller needles, cast on 26 (30, 34) [50 (54, 56)] sts. Work same as Back until piece measures 1¼ (1½, 1½) [2¼ (2½, 2½)]" inc 18 (14, 12) [20 (20, 24)] sts evenly across on last RS row—44 (44, 46) [70 (74, 80)] sts. Change to larger needles. *Next row* (WS) P1, [k1, p2, k1, p1] 0 (0, 0) [2 (2, 3)] times, [k1, p1] 0 (0, 0) [1 (2, 1)] times, k0 (0, 1) [1 (1, 1)], p6, k1, [p1, k1] twice, p3, k1, p1, k1, p8, k1, p1, k1, p3, k1, [p1, k1] twice, p6, k0 (0, 1) [1 (1, 1)], [p1, k1] 0 (0, 0)[1 (2, 1)] times, [p1, k1, p2, k1] 0 (0, 0) [2 (2, 3)] times, p1. *Begin Charts: Row 1* K1, begin charts where indicated and work 0 (0, 0) [10 (12, 15)] sts Chart A, 0 (0, 1) [3 (3, 3)] sts Twisted rib, work as for Back for Chart B through Chart E, work 0 (0, 1) [3 (3, 3)] sts Twisted rib, ending where indicated work 0 (0, 0) [10 (12, 15)] sts Chart F, k1. Continue pats as established, inc 1 st each side (working incs into pat as for Back) on row 3, then every 4th row, 13 (14, 15) [19 (22, 25)] times more—72 (74, 78) [110 (120, 132)] sts. Work even until piece measures 9 (11, 13) [17 (18, 19)]" from beginning, end with a WS row. Bind off.

Finishing

Join right shoulder using 3-needle bind-off.

Neckband

With RS facing and smaller needles, begin at left Front neck, pick up and k10 (12, 12) [14 (15, 15)] sts along left Front neck edge, k10 (12, 14) [16 (20, 20)] from Front holder, pick up and k14 (16, 16) [18 (19, 19)] sts along right Front neck edge, and k26 (32, 34) [40 (46, 46)] sts from Back neck holder (leaving remaining Back sts on hold)—60 (72, 76) [88 (100, 100)] sts. Work in Twisted rib beginning with row 2, until band measures 1½". Bind off in rib.

Back left shoulder band

With smaller needles, and RS facing, begin at neck edge, pick up and k9 (9, 9) [9 (10, 9)] sts along neckband edge, k24 (26, 30) [44 (47, 52)] sts from Back holder—33 (35, 39) [53 (57, 61)] sts. *Row 1* (WS) *K1, p1; rep from *, end k1. *Row 2* *P1, k1 tbl; rep from *, end p1. Work 5 more rows in Twisted rib. Band measures approx 1". Bind off in rib.

Front left shoulder band

With smaller needles and RS facing, beginning at sleeve edge, k24 (26, 30) [44 (47, 52)] sts from Front holder then pick up and k9 (9, 9) [9 (10, 9)] sts along neckband edge—33 (35, 39) [53 (57, 61)] sts. Work 3 rows Twisted rib as for Back band.

Next (buttonhole) row: For Child sizes ONLY: Work 3 (5, 2) sts, [yo (yo, p2tog), p2tog (p2tog, yo), work 4 (4, 6) sts] 5 times, ending last time for size 6 as work 3 sts.

For Men's sizes ONLY: Work 7 sts, [bind off 2 sts, work to 8 (9, 10) sts on needle after bind off] 4 times, bind off 2 sts, work 4 sts.

ALL SIZES: Continue in Twisted rib, casting on 2 sts over bound-off sts for Men's sizes, until same as Back band. Bind off in rib. Lap Front shoulder band over Back shoulder band and sew them together along sleeve edge. Mark Front and Back down 5 (5¼, 5¾) [9 (10, 11)]" from shoulder seam. Sew top of sleeves between markers, centering sleeve on Chart D pattern. Sew side and sleeve seams. Sew on buttons. ∩

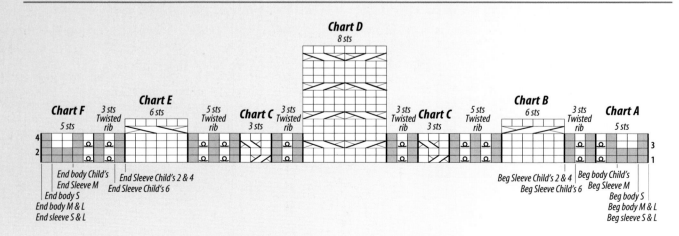

I love this denim yarn because as the garment is washed and worn, it becomes more beautiful and, like a fine wine, improves with age! Don't be put off by the initial stiffness after washing; this soon disappears when worn. This yarn is perfect for children's wear as it is hard-wearing and can be flung in the washing machine with the knowledge that the look is improved rather than destroyed.

What particularly fascinates me is that the process of wearing it makes the dye fade differently depending on the stitch texture so that in time, certain stitches become more enhanced and the appearance of the garment evolves.

Debbie Bliss

denim and cables

Moss st

Row 1 (RS) *K1, p1; rep from*. *Rows 2, 4* K the knit sts and p the purl sts. *Row 3* *P1, k1; rep from*. Rep rows 1-4 for Moss st.

Back

With smaller needles, cast on 111 (123, 135) sts. *Begin Chart A: Row 1* (RS) Work 12-st rep of chart 9 (10, 11) times, work last 3 sts of chart. Continue in chart pat through row 6, then rep rows 1-6 of chart 7 (8, 9) times more. Piece measures approx 5½ (6¼, 7)" from beginning. K 4 rows. Change to larger needles. *Begin Chart pats: Row 1* (RS) Work 4 (10, 16) sts Moss st, 6 sts Chart B, 9 sts Chart C, 15 sts Chart D, 8 sts Chart E, 27 sts Chart F, 8 sts Chart G, 15 sts Chart D, 9 sts Chart H, 6 sts Chart I, end 4 (10, 16) sts in Moss st. Continue pats until piece measures 18¾ (20, 22)" from beginning, end with a WS row.

Shape neck and shoulders

Next row (RS) Continue pats, work 43 (47, 52) sts, join 2nd ball of yarn and bind off 25 (29, 31) sts, work to end. Working both sides at same time, bind off from each neck edge 3 sts once, 2 sts once, AT SAME TIME, after 2 rows of neck shaping have been worked, bind off from each shoulder edge 12 (14, 15) sts once, 13 (14, 16) sts twice.

Pocket linings MAKE 2

With smaller needles, cast on 24 sts. Work 3½ (4¼, 5)" in St st, inc 3 sts across last row—27 sts. Place sts on hold.

Front

Cast on and work Chart A as for back for 35 (41, 47) rows.

Place pocket

Next row (WS) Continue pat, work 12 sts, bind off 27 sts, work to last 39 sts, bind off 27 sts, work to end. *Next row* *Work to bound-off sts, work across sts of pocket lining in chart pats as established; rep from* once more, work to end. Continue pats as for back until piece measures 17¼ (18½, 20½)" from beginning, end with a WS row.

Shape neck

Next row (RS) Continue pats, work 45 (49, 54) sts, join 2nd ball of yarn and bind off center 21 (25, 27) sts, work to end. Working both sides at same time, bind off from each neck edge 3 sts once, 2 sts once. Dec 1 st at each neck edge every other row twice. Work even until same length as back to shoulders. Shape shoulders as for back.

Sleeves

With smaller needles, cast on 59 (61, 63) sts. *Begin Chart A: Row 1* (RS) Begin as indicated, work to end of 12-st rep, then work 12-st rep 4 times, end as indicated.

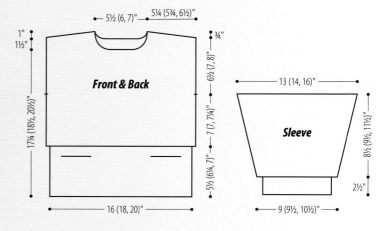

— 5½ (6, 7)" — | — 5¼ (5¾, 6½)" —
1" / 1½" ¾"
17¼ (18½, 20½)" 6½ (7, 8)" 7 (7, 7¼)"
Front & Back
5½ (6¼, 7)"
— 16 (18, 20)" —

— 13 (14, 16)" —
Sleeve
8½ (9¼, 11½)"
2½"
— 9 (9½, 10½)" —

Continue in chart pat through row 6, then rep rows 1-6 of chart twice more. K 4 rows, inc 2 (4, 6) sts on last row—61 (65, 69) sts. Change to larger needles. *Begin Chart pats: Row 1* (RS) Work last 0 (2, 4) sts of Chart I, 9 sts Chart C, 8 sts Chart E, 27 sts Chart F, 8 sts Chart G, 9 sts Chart H, end work first 0 (2, 4) sts of Chart B. Continue in pats as established, AT SAME TIME, inc 1 st each side (working incs into Charts B and I, then into Moss st) every 4th row 2 (0, 3) times, then every 6th row 10 (13, 14) times—85 (91, 103) sts. Work even until piece measures 11 (12, 14)" from beginning. Bind off.

Finishing

Block pieces. Sew right shoulder.

Neckband

With RS facing and smaller needles, begin at left shoulder and pick up and k60 (66, 66) sts evenly along front neck, 39 (45, 45) sts along back neck—99 (111, 111) sts. *Begin rib: Row 1* (WS) K3, *p3, k3; rep from* to end. K the knit sts and p the purl sts until band measures 2", end with a RS row. (*Note* WS of neckband now becomes RS for foldover.) Change to larger needles. *Begin Chart A: Row 1* (RS) Work 12-st rep 8 (9, 9) times, work last 3 sts of chart. Work chart pat as established through row 6, then rep rows 1–6 of chart twice more. Bind off loosely in pat. Sew left shoulder and neckband (reversing seam at upper 2¼" of neckband). Place markers 6½ (7, 8)" down from shoulders on front and back. Sew top of sleeves between markers. Sew pocket linings to WS. Sew side and sleeve seams. ∩

Note Cotton denim yarns will shrink in length when washed. The length measurements in the instructions are after washing. If you are using a denim yarn, measure the length of your swatch before washing and after washing. Divide the after-washing length by the before-washing length. The resulting number should be multiplied by the instruction lengths to arrive at the necessary before-washing lengths.

Skill Intermediate
Fit Oversized
Sizes 6 (8, 10). Shown in 6.
Finished measurements 32 (36, 40)" around and 19¾ (21, 23)" long.
Gauge 43 sts equal 15cm/6" and 36 rows equal 10cm/4" over Charts G, F, and E (after washing), using larger needles.
Yarn 1450 (1720, 2135) yds. Medium weight.
Needles Sizes 3.75 and 4mm/US 5 and 6, *or size to obtain gauge*.
Extras Cable needle (cn). Stitch holder and markers.
Original yarn Rowan Den-M-nit (100% cotton; 1¾ oz/50g, 101 yds/91m).

□ K on RS, p on WS

▨ P on RS, k on WS

⊡ **3MB** With LH needle, pick up strand between st just worked and next st on LH needle; work k1, p1, k1 into strand; turn, p3; turn, k3; turn, p1, p2tog; turn, k2tog; p next st on LH needle, then pass bobble st over p st and off needle.

● **4MB** Work k1, p1, k1, p1 into a st; turn, p4; turn, k4; turn, p4; turn, sl 2, k2tog, then pass 2 sl sts, one at a time, over k2tog and off needle.

▨ **1/1 RPC** Sl 1 to cn, hold to back, k1; p1 from cn.

▨ **1/1 LPC** Sl 1 to cn, hold to front, p1; k1 from cn.

▨ **2/1 LC** Sl 2 to cn, hold to front, k1; k2 from cn.

▨ **2/1 RPC** Sl 1 to cn, hold to back, k2; p1 from cn.

▨ **2/1 LPC** Sl 2 to cn, hold to front, p1; k2 from cn.

▨ **2/2 RC** Sl 2 to cn, hold to back, k2; k2 from cn.

▨ **2/2 LC** Sl 2 to cn, hold to front, k2; k2 from cn.

▨ **3/3 RC** Sl 3 to cn, hold to back, k3; k3 from cn.

▨ **3/3 LC** Sl 3 to cn, hold to front, k3; k3 from cn.

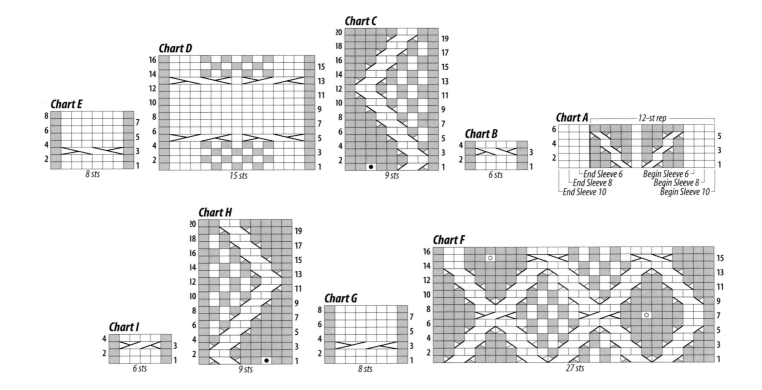

Front & Back Pat Arrangement

4 (10, 16) sts moss st	6 sts Chart I	9 sts Chart H	15 sts Chart D	8 sts Chart G	27 sts Chart F	8 sts Chart E	15 sts Chart D	9 sts Chart C	6 sts Chart B	4 (10, 16) sts moss st

Sleeve Pat Arrangement

0 (2, 4) sts Chart B	9 sts Chart H	8 sts Chart G	27 sts Chart F	8 sts Chart E	9 sts Chart C	0 (2, 4) sts Chart I

denim and cables

cables with heart

*I began where countless designers have journeyed before—in a **Barbara Walker Treasury** with a pattern called 'heart strings.' This pattern reminded me of Celtic knot patterns. I used this as a jumping off point and played with many variations. Using photocopies of the same motif and placing them differently I was able to finally come up with her 'play on hearts.'*

Ann Regis

cables with heart

WOMAN'S PULLOVER

Notes

1 See School, p. 102, for Make 1. **2** Sl sts purl-wise with yarn in back unless otherwise indicated.

Back

Cast on 108 sts. **Foundation row** (WS) P2, k2, p1, k2, [p4, k2, (p2, k2) twice] twice, p4, k2, p1, k2, [p2, k2] twice, p4, k2, [p2, k2] twice, p1, k2, [p4, k2, (p2, k2) twice] twice, p4, k2, p1, k2, p2. **Begin Cable Rib: Row 1** (RS) K2, p2, sl 1, p2, 2/2 LC, [(p2, k2) twice, p2, 2/2 RC] twice, p2, sl 1, [p2, k2] twice, p2, 2/2 RC, [p2, k2] twice, p2, sl 1, [p2, 2/2 LC, (p2, k2) twice] twice, p2, 2/2 RC, p2, sl 1, p2, k2. **Rows 2 and 4** K the knit sts, p the purl sts and the sl sts. **Row 3** K the knit sts, p the purl sts, sl the sl sts. [Rep rows 1–4] 1 (2, 2) times more, then rep rows 1–3 once. **Next row** (WS) K2, k into front and back of next st (inc 1), k1, *p1, k2, p4, [inc 1] twice, p2, k4, k2tog, p4, k2tog, k4, p2, [inc 1] twice, p4, k2, p1*, k10, p4, k10, rep from * to * once, k1, inc 1, k2—114 sts.
Begin chart pats: Row 1 (RS) P5, sl 1, place marker (pm), work 12 sts of Chart A, pm, 14 sts Chart B, pm, 12 sts Chart C, pm, 26 sts Chart D, pm, 12 sts Chart A, pm, 14 sts Chart E, pm, 12 sts Chart C, sl 1, p5. **Row 2** K5, p1, slip marker (sm), work 12 sts of Chart C, sm, 14 sts Chart E, sm, 12 sts Chart A, sm, 26 sts Chart D, sm, 12 sts Chart C, sm, 14 sts Chart B, sm, 12 sts Chart A, p1, k5. Continue in pats as established, inc 0 (1, 1) st each side (working incs into rev St st) every 4th row 0 (2, 4) times—122 (126, 130) sts (including 8 sts inc'd on row 3 of Chart D). Work even until piece measures approx 17 (17½, 17½)" from beginning, end with row 24 of Chart D.
Shape armholes
Bind off 4 (5, 6) sts at beginning of next 2 rows—106 (108, 110) sts. Work even until 32 rows of Chart D have been worked 4 times from beginning.
Sizes M (L) only Work 4 rows more in all pats and for Chart D only, work chart rows 29-32.
All Sizes: Next row (RS) Bind off 42 (43, 44) sts, place center 22 sts on hold, join 2nd ball of yarn and bind off rem 42 (43, 44) sts. Armhole measures approx 7 (7½, 7½)".

Front

Work as for Back.

Sleeves

Cast on 46 sts. **Foundation row** (WS) P2, k2, p4, k2, p2, k2, p1, k2, p2, k2, p4, k2, p2, k2, p1, k2, p2, k2, p4, k2, p2. **Begin Cable Rib: Row 1** (RS) K2, p2, 2/2 RC, p2, k2, p2, sl 1, p2, k2, p2, 2/2 RC, p2, k2, p2, sl 1, p2, k2, p2, 2/2 LC, p2, k2. **Rows 2 and 4** K the knit sts, p the purl sts and the sl sts. **Row 3** K the knit sts, p the purl sts

Skill Intermediate
Fit Loose
Sizes S(M,L). Shown in Small.
Sweater measures 44 (46, 48)" around and 26½ (27½, 27½)" long.
Gauge 14 sts and 18 rows equal 10cm/4" over St st.
Yarn 1645 (1775, 1825) yds. Bulky weight.
Needles 6mm/US 10, *or size to obtain gauge.*
6mm/US 10 circular, 60cm/24" long.
Extras Cable needle (cn). Stitch holders and markers.
Original yarn Classic Elite's Stonington (100% superwash wool; 3½ ozs/ 100g, approx 137 yds/124m).

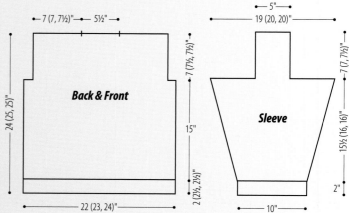

and sl the sl sts. Rep rows 1–4 once more, then work rows 1-2 once. **Next row** (RS) K2, p2, k4, p2, k2, p2, sl 1, p2, k2, p2, [k1, M1] 4 times, p2, k2, p2, sl 1, p2, k2, p2, k4, p2, k2—50 sts. **Next row** (WS) K2, inc 1, k1, p4, k2tog, k4, p1, k2, p2, [inc 1] twice, p4, M1, p4, [inc 1] twice, p2, k2, p1, k4, k2tog, p4, k1, inc 1, k2—55 sts.
Begin chart pats: Row 1 (RS) Work 14 sts Chart B, pm, 27 sts Chart F, pm, 14 sts Chart E. **Row 2** Work 14 sts Chart E, sm, 27 sts Chart F, sm, 14 sts Chart B. Continue in pats as established, AT SAME TIME, inc 1 st each side (working incs into rev St st) every 4th row 1 (3, 3) times, every 6th row 13 times—83 (87, 87) sts. Work even until piece measures 17½ (18, 18)" from beginning, end with a WS row.
Shape saddle shoulder
Bind off 27 (29, 29) sts at beginning of next 2 rows—29 sts. Work even until saddle measures 7 (7, 7½)". Bind off.

Finishing

Block pieces. Sew sleeves to body as follows: Sew sides of saddle shoulder to front and back shoulder sts of body, then sew bound-off sleeve sts to armhole. Sew bound-off body sts to side edges of sleeves. Sew side and sleeve seams.
Neckband
With RS facing and circular needle, begin at front neck holder and work as follows: K22, then pick up and k22 sts along top of right saddle shoulder, k22 from back holder, pick up and k22 sts along top of left saddle shoulder—88 sts. Pm, join and work in rnds as follows: **Rnd 1** P1, [k2, p2] twice, pm, 2/2 RC, pm, *[p2, k2] 4 times, p2, pm, 2/2 RC, pm; rep from* twice more, [p2, k2] twice, p1. **Rnds 2–4** K the knit sts and p the purl sts. Rep rnds 1–4 once more, then rep rnd 1 once. **Next (dec) rnd** Rep rnd 2, working p2tog in each p2 around. Bind off. ∩

□ K on RS, p on WS

▨ P on RS, k on WS

▼ Knit into front, back, front of st

▼ Sl 1 purl-wise with yarn in back

M Make 1 knit

⬕ **DEC 4** Sl 3 knit-wise, one at a time to RH needle; *pass 2nd st on RH needle over last st (center st) and off needle; sl center st back to LH needle; sl 2nd st on LH needle over center st and off needle;* sl center st back to RH needle; rep from * to * once; k1

▪ No stitches exist in these areas of chart

⬚ **2/1 RPC** Sl 1 to cn, hold to back, k2; p1 from cn.

⬚ **2/1 LPC** Sl 2 to cn, hold to front, p1; k2 from cn.

⬚ **2/2 RC** Sl 2 to cn, hold to back, k2; k2 from cn.

⬚ **2/2 LC** Sl 2 to cn, hold to front, k2; k2 from cn.

⬚ **2/2 RPC** Sl 2 to cn, hold to back, k2; p2 from cn.

⬚ **2/2 LPC** Sl 2 to cn, hold to front, p2; k2 from cn.

⬚ **2/2 Rib RC** Sl 2 to cn, hold to back, p2; p1, k1 from cn.

⬚ **2/2 Rib LC** Sl 2 to cn, hold to front, k1, p1; p2 from cn.

⬚ **2/3 RPC** Sl 3 to cn, hold to back, k2; p3 from cn.

⬚ **2/3 LPC** Sl 2 to cn, hold to front, p3; k2 from cn.

Chart A
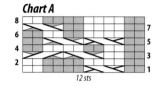
12 sts

Chart C
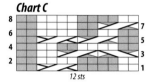
12 sts

Chart B
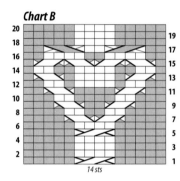
14 sts

Chart E
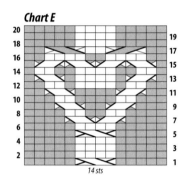
14 sts

Chart D
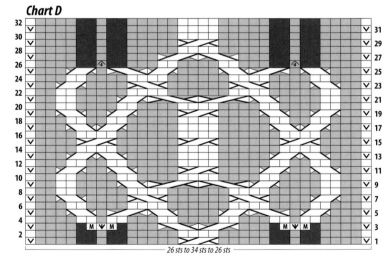
26 sts to 34 to 26 sts

Chart F
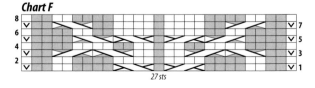
27 sts

Sleeve Pat Arrangement

14 sts	27 sts	14 sts
Chart E	Chart F	Chart B

Back Pat Arrangement

5 sts rev St st + 0 (2, 4)	Sl 1 (RS) P1 (WS)	12 sts Chart C	14 sts Chart E	12 sts Chart A	26 to 34 to 26 sts Chart D	12 sts Chart C	14 sts Chart B	12 sts Chart A	Sl 1 (RS) P1 (WS)	5 sts rev St st + 0 (2, 4)

It took me quite a few tries to get the heart cable to look just the way I wanted it. Then I couldn't stop with just the cardigan, so along came the hat and the teddy bear sweater, and of course, his hat!

Linda Cyr

CHILD'S CARDIGAN

Notes

1 See School, p. 102 for M1, yo before a k and p st, and tassels. **2** Sweater is knit in one piece to underarm, then divided into Fronts and Back. **3** Sl sts purlwise with yarn in back unless indicated otherwise.

Seed st pat *OVER ANY NUMBER OF STS*

Row 1 (RS) *K1, p1; rep from*. *Row 2* K the purl sts and p the knit sts. Rep Row 2 for Seed st.

Body

Cast on 182 (190, 198) sts. *Begin Charts A and B, Rib pat, and 6-st Front Band pat: Row 1* (RS) Sl 1, [k1, p1] twice, sl 1 (6-st front band), k0 (2, 2), p2, *work 4 sts Chart A, [p2, k2] 4 times, p2, 4 sts Chart B, [p2, k2] 6 (6, 7) times, p2, 4 sts Chart A, [p2, k2] 4 times, p2, 4 sts Chart B*, [p2, k2] 2 (3, 3) times, p2, rep from * to * once, p2, k0 (2, 2), sl 1, [k1, p1] twice, sl 1 (6-st front band). *Row 2* P2, [k1, p1] twice, p0 (2, 2), k2, *work 4 sts Chart B, [k2, p2] 4 times, k2, 4 sts Chart A, [k2, p2] 6 (6, 7) times, k2, 4 sts Chart B, [k2, p2] 4 times, k2, 4 sts Chart A*, [k2, p2] 2 (3, 3) times, k2, rep from * to * once, k2, p0 (2, 2), p2, [k1, p1] twice. Work 0 (2, 2) rows more in pats as established. Work Eyelet Buttonhole (see illustrations, p. 91) over next 3 rows. Continue to work buttonholes every 2½ (2¾, 2¾)" 4 times more, AT SAME TIME, continue in pats as follows: Work 10 (4, 8) rows more in pats as established. *Dec row* (WS) Work 12 (14, 14) sts, k2tog, work 14 sts, k2tog, work 4 sts, k2tog, work 22 (22, 26) sts, k2tog, work 4 sts, k2tog, work 14 sts, k2tog, work 18 (22, 22) sts, k2tog, work 14 sts, k2tog, work 4 sts, k2tog, work 22 (22, 26) sts, k2tog, work 4 sts, k2tog, work 14 sts, k2tog, work 12 (14, 14) sts—170 (178, 186) sts.

Begin Chart C and Seed st pat: Row 1 (RS) Work 6 sts of front band, 2 (4, 4) sts in Seed st, *4 sts Chart A, 16 sts Chart C, 4 sts Chart B,* 24 (24, 28) sts in Seed st, rep from * to * once, 10 (14, 14) sts in Seed st, rep from * to * once, 24 (24, 28) sts in Seed st, rep from * to * once, 2 (4, 4) sts in Seed st, 6 sts front band. Continue in pats as established until piece measures 6½ (7, 7)" from beginning, end with a RS row.

Divide for fronts and back

Next row (WS) Work 39 (41, 43) sts (left front), bind off 10 sts (underarm), work until there are 72 (76, 80) sts for back, bind off 10 sts (underarm), work to end. Work 39 (41, 43) sts of right front and place rem sts on hold.

Right Front

Work even until armhole measures 3¾ (4¾, 5¼)", end with a RS row.

Shape shoulder

Next row (WS) Bind off 21 (21, 23) sts, work to end. Place rem 18 (20, 20) sts on hold.

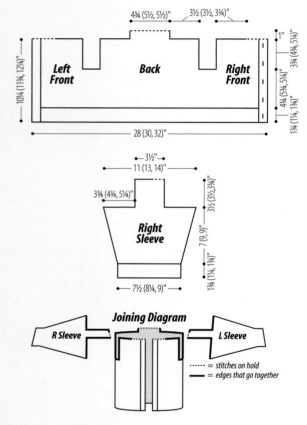

= stitches on hold
= edges that go together

Back

With RS facing, join yarn at underarm edge and work even on 72 (76, 80) sts until armhole measures same length as right front to shoulders, end with a WS row.

Shape shoulders

Bind off 21 (21, 23) sts at beginning of next 2 rows—30 (34, 34) sts.

Shape neck

Work 6 rows even. Place sts on hold.

Left Front

With RS facing, join yarn at underarm and work as for right front, reversing shaping by binding off for shoulder at beginning of a RS row.

Right Sleeve

Cast on 42 (46, 50) sts. *Begin Charts A and B and Rib pat: Row 1* (RS) P2 (0, 2), [k2, p2] 2 (3, 3) times, 4 sts Chart A, [p2, k2] 3 times, p2, 4 sts Chart B, [p2, k2] 2 (3, 3) times, p2 (0, 2). Work 13 (9, 13) rows more in pats as established, dec 1 st each side on last row—40 (44, 48) sts.

Sizes Child's 18/24 months (3/4, 5/6). Shown in 3/4.
Finished measurements Sweater measures 27 (29, 31)" around, when buttoned, and 10¼ (11¾, 12¼)" long. Hat measures 17" around.
Gauge 20 sts and 32 rows equal 10cm/4" over Seed st.
Yarn Child's cardigan 575 (730, 820) yds. Child's hat 210 yds. Teddy bear hat and sweater 110 yds each (instructions on p. 93).
All medium weight.
Needles Size 3½mm/US4, *or size to obtain gauge.*
Buttons Five 15mm/⅝" buttons.
Extras Cable needle (cn).
Stitch markers and holders.
Original yarn Dale of Norway Freestyle (100% machine wash- able wool, 1¾ oz/50g, approx 104 yds/95m).

cables with heart

Begin Chart C and Seed st pat: Row 1 (RS) Work 9 (11, 13) sts in Seed st, 4 sts Chart A,14 sts Chart C, 4 sts Chart B, 9 (11, 13) sts in Seed st. Continue in pats as established, AT SAME TIME, inc 1 st each side (working incs into Seed st) every 4th row 5 (6, 6) times, every 6th row 5 (7, 7) times—60 (70, 74) sts. Work even until piece measures 8¾ (10¼, 10¾)" from beginning, end with a WS row.

Shape saddle shoulder

Bind off 18 (23, 25) sts at beginning of next 2 rows—24 sts. Work even for 3½ (3½, 3¾)", end with a RS row. **Next row** (WS) Bind off 7 sts, work to end. Place rem 17 sts on hold.

Left Sleeve

Work as for right sleeve, working last row of saddle shoulder on a RS row as follows: **Next row** (RS) Bind off 7 sts, work to end. Place rem 17 sts on hold.

Finishing

Sew sleeves to body as follows: Line up side edges of sleeve's saddle shoulders to 21 (21, 23) bound-off sts of front and back and sew back neck extension to the 7 sts bound off at top of saddle shoulders. Sew bound-off sts at each side of sleeve's saddle shoulder to armholes. Sew sleeve seams.

Neckband

With RS facing, join yarn and work sts from holders as follows: on right front, work 6 sts of front band, k0 (2, 2), p2, 4 sts Chart A, p2, k2, p2tog; on right sleeve, p1, 4 sts Chart A, [p2, k2] 3 times; on back, p2, k2, p2, 4 sts Chart B, [p2, k2] 2 (3, 3) times, p2, 4 sts Chart A, p2, k2, p2; on left sleeve, [k2, p2] 3 times, 4 sts Chart B, p1; on left front, p2tog, k2, p2, 4 sts Chart B, p2, k0 (2, 2), 6 sts front band—98 (106, 106) sts. Work 3 rows even. **Next row** (RS) Work pats and work p2tog on all p2's—79 (86, 86) sts. Work 3 rows more. Bind off in pat. Sew on buttons.

HAT

Front

Cast on 46 sts. **Begin Charts A and B and Rib pat: Row 1** (RS) [K2, p2] 3 times, 4 sts Chart A, [p2, k2] 3 times, p2, 4 sts Chart B, [p2, k2] 3 times. Work 6 rows more in pats as established. **Next row** (WS) Work 16 sts in pat, M1, work 14 sts, M1, work 16 sts—48 sts. **Begin Chart C and Seed st: Row 1** (RS) Work 12 sts in Seed st, 4 sts Chart A, 16 sts Chart C, 4 sts Chart B, 12 sts in Seed st. Continue in pats as established until piece measures 7" from beginning. Bind off.

Back

Work as for front.

Finishing

Sew front and back tog along sides and top. Make 2 tassels, each 4" long, and secure to each corner.

Eyelet Buttonhole rows

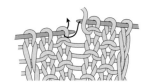

Row 1 (RS) Sl 1, k1, p1, *yo, k1 (as shown)*, p1, sl 1, work in pat to end.

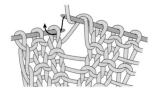

Row 2 (WS) Work to last 7 sts, p2, *k1, then with yarn in front, sl yo to RH needle, then yo again (as shown)*, p1, k1, p1.

Row 3 Sl 1, k1, sl 1 knitwise, *k the 2 yo's tog, leaving them on LH needle (as shown)*, pass the sl st over st just made on RH needle, then k the yo's tog with next st on LH needle, p1, sl 1, work to end.

☐ K on RS, p on WS

▨ P on RS, k on WS

[◯▶◀◯] Sl 2, pass 2nd st on RH needle over first st; sl first st on RH needle back to LH needle and pass 2nd st on LH needle over first st (2 sts dec'd); yo, k1, yo. On next row, p yo's through back loop (tbl)

[◯◀▶◯] Sl 1, pass 2nd st on LH needle over first st; sl first st on LH needle to RH needle; pass 2nd st on RH needle over first st (2 sts dec'd); sl first st on RH needle back to LH needle; yo, k1, yo. On next row, p yo's tbl

▨ **1/1 RC** Sl 1 to cn, hold to back, k1; k1 from cn.

▨ **1/1 LC** Sl 1 to cn, hold to front, k1; k1 from cn.

▨ **1/1 RPC** Sl 1 to cn, hold to back, k1; p1 from cn.

▨ **1/1 LPC** Sl 1 to cn, hold to front, p1; k1 from cn.

▨ **2/1 RPC** Sl 1 to cn, hold to back, k2; p1 from cn.

▨ **2/1 LPC** Sl 2 to cn, hold to front, p1; k2 from cn.

▨ **2/2 RC** Sl 2 to cn, hold to back, k2; k2 from cn.

▨ **2/2 LC** Sl 2 to cn, hold to front, k2; k2 from cn.

Chart A

4 sts

Chart B

4 sts

Chart C

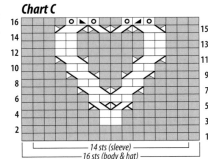

14 sts (sleeve)
16 sts (body & hat)

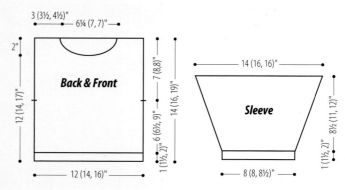

3 (3½, 4½)" · 6¼ (7, 7)"

Back & Front

Sleeve

14 (16, 16)"

12 (14, 17)" · 7 (8,8)" · 14 (16, 19)" · 6 (6½, 9)" · 1 (1½, 2)"

8½ (11, 12)" · 1 (1½, 2)"

12 (14, 16)" · 8 (8, 8½)"

Sue Mink

cables with heart

Skill Intermediate

Fit Loose

Sizes Child's 2 (4/6, 8). Shown in 4/6.

Finished measurements 24 (28, 32)" around and 14 (16, 19)" long.

Gauge 11 sts and 18 rows equal 10cm/4" over Seed st with larger needles.

Yarns 440 (600, 765). Bulky weight.

Needles One pair each sizes 4.5 and 5.5mm/US 7 and 9, *or size to obtain gauge.*
Size 4.5mm/US 7 circular, 40 cm/16" long.

Extras Cable needle (cn). Stitch markers.

Original yarn Cleckheaton/Plymouth's Antartica (100% wool; 3½ ozs/100g, approx 100 yds/90m).

I started out wanting to make a heart in a combination of knit and purl stitches. From there, I worked with a heart motif in Barbara Walker's Charted Knitting Designs and adapted it. I threw in the hugs and kisses cables for good measure. I really wanted to make a sweater a grandmother would love to make for a special grandchild.

CHILD'S PULLOVER

Notes

1 See *School*, p. 102, for M1 (right- and left-slanting),ssk, ssp and yo before a k and p st. **2** Keep 1 st at each edge in St st.

Seed st *OVER ANY NUMBER OF STS*

Row 1 (RS) *K1, p1; rep from*. *Row 2* K the purl sts and p the knit sts. Rep Row 2 for seed st.

Back

With smaller needles, cast on 43 (47, 53) sts. Work 1 (1½, 2)" in k1, p1 rib, inc 6 (8, 8) sts evenly across last (WS) row—49 (55, 61) sts. Change to larger needles.
Begin Chart A and Seed st pat: Row 1 (RS) K1, work 5 (8, 11) sts in Seed st, k1, p2, place marker (pm), 8 sts Chart A, pm, p15, pm, 8 sts Chart A, pm, p2, k1, 5 (8, 11) sts in Seed st, k1. *Row 2* P1, work 5 (8, 11) sts in Seed st, p1, k2, slip marker (sm), 8 sts Chart A, sm, k15, sm, 8 sts Chart A, sm, k2, p1, 5 (8, 11) sts in Seed st, p1. Work 3 (3, 1) rows more in pats as established. *Begin Chart B: Next row* (WS) Work pats as established to 2nd marker, work Row 1 of Chart B over 15 sts, work in pat to end. Work through row 15 of Chart B. Work 5 (9, 5) rows more, working center 15 sts in rev St st. Rep from* 2 (2, 3) times more, then work center 15 sts in rev St st until piece measures 14 (16, 19)" from beginning. Bind off.

Front

Work as for back, except work center 15 sts as follows: Work 7 (5, 9) rows in rev St st after ribbing. *Work 15 rows of Chart B, work 9 (5, 7) rows in rev St st. Rep from* 1 (2, 2) times more, then work center 15 sts in rev St st until piece measures 12 (14, 17)" from beginning, end with a WS row.

Shape neck

Next row (RS) Work 20 (22, 25) sts, join 2nd ball of yarn and bind off center 9 (11, 11) sts, work to end. Working both sides at same time, bind off from each neck edge 2 sts twice—16 (18, 21) sts each side. Work even until piece measures same length as back to shoulder. Bind off all sts.

Sleeves

With smaller needles, cast on 27 (27, 29) sts. Work 1 (1½, 2)" in k1, p1 rib, inc 3 sts on last (WS) row—30 (30, 32) sts. Change to larger needles. *Begin Chart A and Seed st pat: Row 1* (RS) K1, work 7 (7, 8) sts in Seed st, k1, p2, pm, 8 sts Chart A, pm, p2, k1, 7 (7, 8) sts in Seed st, k1. Continue in pats as established, AT SAME TIME, inc 1 st each side (working incs into Seed st inside 1 St st selvage each side) every 6th row 5 (8, 7) times — 40 (46, 46) sts. Work even until sleeve measures 9½ (12½, 14)" from beginning. Bind off.

Finishing

Block pieces. Sew shoulders.

Neckband

With RS facing and circular needle, begin at left shoulder and pick up and k25 (27, 27) sts along front neck, and 17 (19, 19) sts along back neck—42 (46, 46) sts. Pm, join and work in rnds of k1, p1 rib for 2". Bind off loosely. Fold neckband in half and sew to WS.

Place markers 7 (8, 8)" down from shoulders on front and back for armholes. Sew top of sleeves between markers. Sew side and sleeve seams. ∩

☐ K on RS, p on WS

⬛ P on RS, k on WS

ⓨ Make 1 knit (right-slanting)

ⓧ Make 1 knit (left-slanting)

ⓨ Make 1 purl (right-slanting)

ⓧ Make 1 purl (left-slanting)

ⓥ Yo, p1, yo

Ⓠ K1 through back loop

◿ P3tog

◣ Ssk

◿ K2tog

◢ Ssp

◿ P2tog

▱ **2/2 RC** Sl 2 to cn, hold to back, k2; k2 from cn.

▱ **2/2 LC** Sl 2 to cn, hold to front, k2; k2 from cn.

Chart B

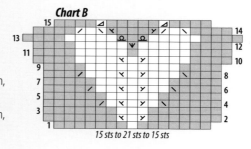

15 sts to 21 sts to 15 sts

Chart A

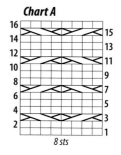

8 sts

TEDDY BEAR SWEATER

Front

Cast on 34 sts. *Begin Charts A and B and Rib pat: Row 1* (RS) P2, k2, p2, 4 sts Chart A, [p2, k2] 3 times, p2, 4 sts Chart B, p2, k2, p2. Continue in pats as established until piece measures ¾", end with a WS row.

Begin Chart C and Seed st: Row 1 (RS) Work Seed st over 6 sts, 4 sts Chart A, 14 sts Chart C, 4 sts Chart B, Seed st over 6 sts. Continue in pats as established until piece measures 5" from beginning, end with a WS row. Bind off 10 sts at beginning of next 2 rows—14 sts. Place sts on hold.

Back

Work as for front.

Sleeves

Cast on 24 sts. *Begin Charts A and B and Rib pat: Row 1* (RS) [P2, k2] twice, p2, 4 sts Chart A, [p2, k2] twice, p2. Continue in pats as established until piece measures ½" end with a WS row.

Begin Seed st: Row 1 (RS) Work Seed st over 10 sts, 4 sts Chart A, Seed st over 10 sts. Work in established pats until piece measures 2½" from beginning, end with a WS row.

Shape saddle shoulder
Bind off 9 sts at beginning of next 2 rows—6 sts. Work 4" even. Place sts on hold.

Finishing

Sew one sleeve to body as follows: Sew sides of saddle shoulder to front and back shoulders, then sew bound-off sleeve sts to armholes. Sew side and sleeve seams. Sew 2nd saddle shoulder to back shoulder and armhole only.
Neckband
With RS facing, begin at right saddle and work across sts on hold as follows: P1, M1, k1, [p2, k2] 9 times, p1, M1, p1—42 sts. *Next row* (WS) K1, [k2, p2] 10 times, k1. Continue in rib pat as established until neckband measures ½". Bind off loosely in rib. Sew rem saddle shoulder to front shoulder and armhole. Sew side and sleeve seams.

TEDDY BEAR HAT

Cast on 49 sts. *Begin Charts A and B and Rib pat: Row 1* (RS) [K1, p1] 3 times, 4 sts Chart A, [p1, k1] twice, p1, 4 sts Chart B, [p1, k1] 5 times, p1, 4 sts Chart A, [p1, k1] twice, p1, 4 sts Chart B, [p1, k1] 3 times. Continue in pat as established until piece measures ½", end with a WS row. *Next row* Continue cable patterns and begin working Seed st over all rib sections. Work in established pat until piece measures 2½" from beginning. Bind off.

Finishing

Fold hat in half with RS together, sew top and side seams. Make two 1½" long tassels, attach to corners.

Size To fit a 10-12" teddy bear.
Measurements Sweater measures 11½" around chest, 5½" long.
Materials See p. 90.
Gauge See p. 90.

☐ K on RS, p on WS

▨ P on RS, k on WS

⊡⬤⬛⬤⊡ Sl 2, pass 2nd st on RH needle over first st; sl first st on RH needle back to LH needle and pass 2nd st on LH needle over first st (2 sts dec'd); yo, k1, yo. On next row, p yo's through back loop (tbl)

⊡⬤◢⬤⊡ Sl 1, pass 2nd st on LH needle over first st; sl first st on LH needle to RH needle; pass 2nd st on RH needle over first st (2 sts dec'd); sl first st on RH needle back to LH needle; yo, k1, yo. On next row, p yo's tbl

▨◿ **1/1 RC** Sl 1 to cn, hold to back, k1; k1 from cn.

◺▨ **1/1 LC** Sl 1 to cn, hold to front, k1; k1 from cn.

▨◿ **1/1 RPC** Sl 1 to cn, hold to back, k1; p1 from cn.

◺▨ **1/1 LPC** Sl 1 to cn, hold to front, p1; k1 from cn.

◺◿ **2/1 RPC** Sl 1 to cn, hold to back, k2; p1 from cn.

◺◿ **2/1 LPC** Sl 2 to cn, hold to front, p1; k2 from cn.

◺◿ **2/2 RC** Sl 2 to cn, hold to back, k2; k2 from cn.

◺◿ **2/2 LC** Sl 2 to cn, hold to front, k2; k2 from cn.

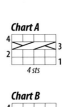

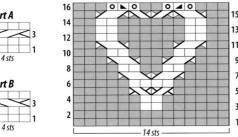

Chart A

4 sts

Chart B

4 sts

Chart C

14 sts

Gauge is determined by four variables: hands, pattern stitch, yarn, and needles. Knitter's editor, Nancy Thomas issued the ultimate gauge challenge: design and size these family vests by changing two of these variables—yarn and needles. Armed with a stash of various needles and two weights of the same type of yarn, I set forward with this task. These vests are the result of numerous swatches and an enlightening exercise. Trust me—gauge is important!

Kathy Zimmerman

copycat vests

BOTH
Skill Intermediate
CHILD'S
Fit Loose
Sizes 4 (6/8, 10/12). Shown in 6/8.
Finished measurements 29 (33½, 37½)" around and 17¾ (19, 21¼)" long.
Gauge 27 sts and 34 rows equal 10cm/4" over rev St st, using larger needles.
32 sts of Cable chart to 9.5cm/3¾", using larger needles.
Yarn 725 (900, 1150) yds. Light weight.
Needles Sizes 3.5 and 4mm/US 4 and 6, *or size to obtain gauge*.
Size 3.5mm/US 4 circular, 40cm/16" long.
Extras Cable needle (cn).
Stitch holders and markers.

ADULT'S
Fit Standard
Sizes S (M, L/1X). Shown in Medium.
Finished measurements 39 (45, 51)" around and 22½ (24, 26½)" long.
Gauge 19 sts and 27 rows equal 10cm/4" over rev St st, using larger needles.
32 sts of Cable chart to 12.5cm/5", using larger needles.
Yarn 810 (1000, 1250) yds. Medium weight.
Needles Sizes 4 and 5mm/US 6 and 8, *or size to obtain gauge* .
Size 4mm/US 6 circular, 40cm/16" long.
Extras Cable needle (cn).
Stitch holders and markers.
Original yarn Child's:Plymouth Encore DK (75% acrylic, 25% wool; 1¾ oz/50g, 150 yds/135m) Adult's: Plymouth Encore (75% acrylic, 25% wool; 3½ oz/100g, 200 yds/180m).

Notes

1 See *School*, p. 102, for ssk and 3-needle bind-off. **2** Instructions are for Child and Adult vests. Size differences occur because of different yarn weights and needle sizes. **3** Length measurements for child are given in parentheses; adult's measurements follow in brackets. **4** For ease in working, circle numbers that pertain to your size.

Back

(*Note* Inc 1 by k into front and back of a st.)
With smaller needles, cast on 109 (121, 133) sts. *Begin rib: Row 1* (WS) [P1, k3, p2] 1 (0, 1) time, *k1, p2, k3, p1, k3, p2; rep from* 7 (9, 9) times more, end k1, [p2, k3, p1] 1 (0, 1) time. *Row 2* K the knit sts and p the purl sts. Rep last row 6 times more. *Next (inc) row* (WS) *For sizes 4/Small only* P1, k3, *p2, inc 1, p2, k3, p1, k3*, rep between *'s 7 times more, p2, inc 1, p2, k3, p1—118 sts. *For sizes 6-8/ Med only* Inc 1, p2, k3, p1, k3, work between *'s of Sizes 4/Small a total of 9 times, p2, inc 1—132 sts. *For sizes 10-12/Large only* P1, inc 1, k2, work between *'s of Sizes 4/Small a total of 10 times, p2, inc 1, p2, k2, inc 1, p1—146 sts. *For all sizes* Change to larger needles. *Begin cable chart: Row 1* (RS) Work 4 (11, 18) sts in rev St st, [32 sts of chart, 7 sts rev St st] twice, 32 sts of chart, 4 (11, 18) sts in rev St st. Continue in pat as established until 80 (86, 96) chart rows have been worked and piece measures approx (10½, 11, 12¼)" [13¼, 14, 15½]" from beginning.
Shape armholes
Bind off 8 (9, 10) sts at beginning of next 2 rows, 2 sts at beginning of next 6 (8, 10) rows, 1 st at beginning of next 4 (6, 6) rows—86 (92, 100) sts. Work even until 54 (60, 68) rows have been worked above beginning of armhole shaping. Armhole measures approx (6¼, 7, 8)" [8¼, 9, 10]".
Shape neck
Next row (RS) Continue pat, work 25 (27, 28) sts, join 2nd ball of yarn and bind off 36 (38, 44) sts, work to end. Working both sides at same time, bind off from each neck edge 2 sts once, 1 st once. Work 3 rows even. Armhole measures approx (7¼, 8, 9)" [9¼, 10, 11]". Place rem 22 (24, 25) sts each side on hold.

Front

Work as for back until same length as back to underarm. Mark center 2 sts.
Shape armholes and V-neck
Note Work neck decs on RS rows as follows: Work to last 3 sts of left front, k2tog, k1; on right front, k1, ssk, work to end.
Next row (RS) Continue pat, bind off 8 (9, 10) sts, work to marked sts and place

them on hold, join 2nd ball of yarn and work to end. Work both sides at same time and continue to shape armhole as for back, AT SAME TIME, dec 1 st at each neck edge every other row 17 (18, 20) times, then every 4th row 3 (3, 4) times—22 (24, 25) sts. Work even until armhole measures same as back to shoulder. Place sts on hold.

Finishing

Block pieces. Join shoulders, using 3-needle bind-off.
Neckband
With RS facing and circular needle, begin at left shoulder and pick up and k48 (56, 64) sts evenly along left front neck, k1 from center front holder, place marker (pm), k1, pick up and k48 (56, 64) sts along right front neck, 53 (53, 57) sts along back neck—151 (167, 187) sts. Pm, join and work as follows: *Rnd 1* [K1, p1, k2] 0 (0, 1) time, [p3, k1, p3, k2, p1, k2] 4 (4, 5) times, [p3, k1] 0 (2, 0) times, k1, sl marker, k1, [k2, p1, k2] 1 (0, 1) time, k0 (1, 0), [p3, k1, p3, k2, p1, k2] 8 (9, 9) times, [p3, k1] 0 (0, 2) times. *Rnd 2* Rib as established to 2 sts before center front marker, k2tog, sl marker, ssk, rib to end. Rep rnd 2 until rib measures 1". Bind off in rib, working decs on bind-off rnd.
Armbands
With RS facing and smaller needles, pick up and k109 (121, 133) sts evenly around armhole edge. Rib back and forth as for back for 1". Bind off in rib. Sew side seams, including armbands. ∩

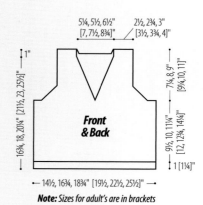

5¼, 5½, 6½" 2½, 2¾, 3"
[7, 7½, 8¾]" [3½, 3¾, 4]"

1"

16¾, 18, 20¼" [21½, 23, 25½]"

7¼, 8, 9"
[9¼, 10, 11]"

9½, 10, 11¼"
[12, 12¾, 14¼]"

Front & Back

1 [1¼]"

← 14½, 16¾, 18¾" [19½, 22½, 25½]" →

Note: *Sizes for adult's are in brackets*

☐ K on WS, p on WS

▨ P on WS, k on WS

⧄ **1/1 RC** Sl 1 to cn, hold to back, k1; k1 from cn.

⧅ **1/1 LC** Sl 1 to cn, hold to front, k1; k1 from cn.

⧄ **1/1 RPC** Sl 1 to cn, hold to back, k1; p1 from cn.

⧅ **1/1 LPC** Sl 1 to cn, hold to front, p1; k1 from cn.

⧄ **3/1 RC** Sl 1 to cn, hold to back, k3; k1 from cn.

⧅ **3/1 LC** Sl 3 to cn, hold to front, k1; k3 from cn.

⧄ **3/1 RPC** Sl 1 to cn, hold to back, k3; p1 from cn.

⧅ **3/1 LPC** Sl 3 to cn, hold to front, p1; k3 from cn.

⧄ **3/3 RC** Sl 3 to cn, hold to back, k3; k3 from cn.

⧅ **3/3 LC** Sl 3 to cn, hold to front, k3; k3 from cn.

Cable Chart

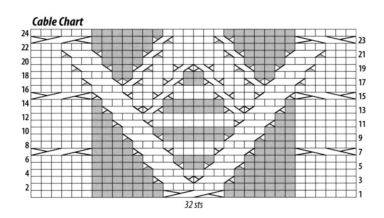

32 sts

Front/Back Pat Arrangement

4 (11, 18) sts Rev St st	32 sts Cable Chart	7 sts Rev St st	32 sts Cable Chart	7 sts Rev St st	32 sts Cable Chart	4 (11, 18) sts Rev St st

copycat vests

tennis for two

I enjoy putting a new spin on tried and true classics. The bold textures of the large cable and seed stitch rib patternwork combine with traditional rope cables and striped ribs to produce crisp, detailed lines. This duo provides a fresh approach to the classic tennis sweater, an updated "Gatsby" look, incorporating both the style and comfort required for today's activewear.

Kathy Zimmerman

tennis for two

Striped rib pat *OVER ODD NUMBER OF STS*
Row 1 (RS) With MC, *k1, p1; rep from *, end k1.
Rows 2–4 Rib 3 rows. *Rows 5, 6* With A, k 1 row, then rib 1 row. *Rows 7, 8* With B, rep rows 5, 6.
Rows 9, 10 With A, rep rows 5, 6. *Rows 11–14* With MC, k 1 row, then rib 3 rows.

Seed st rib *MULTIPLE OF 6 STS PLUS 3*
Row 1 (RS)*P3, k3; rep from *, end p3. *Row 2* K3, *p1, k1, p1, k3; rep from * to end. Rep rows 1-2 for Seed st rib.

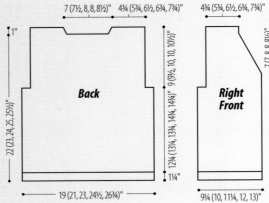

Note
See *School*, p. 102 for 3-needle bind-off, 3-row buttonhole, and ssk.

Skill Intermediate
Fit Loose
Sizes *Cardigan:* S (M, L, 1X, 2X).
Vest: S (M/L, 1X).
Both: Shown in Medium.
Finished measurements
Cardigan: 39 (42½, 47, 50, 54)" at underarm (buttoned) and 23 (24, 25, 26, 26½)" long.
Vest: 38½ (45½, 52½)" at underarm and 25 (26, 27)" long.
Gauge *Both:* 27 sts and 29 rows to 10cm/4" in Seed st rib, using size 4mm/US 6 needles. 20 sts of Chart B to 8cm/3¼".
Yarn *Cardigan:* 1525 (1730, 1945, 2100, 2345) yds in Ecru (MC); 108 yds each in Light Olive (A) and Bluebell (B). Medium Weight.
Vest: 1140 (1400, 1685) yds in Beige (MC); 108 yds each in Navy (A) and Light Olive (B). Medium Weight.
Needles *Both:* One pair each sizes 3.25mm and 4mm/US 3 and 6 needles, *or size needed to obtain gauge.* Size 3.25mm/US 3 circular needle, 80cm/32" (cardigan) and 60cm/24" (vest).
Buttons *Cardigan:* 7 (7, 7, 8, 8) 20mm/¾".
Extras Cable needle (cn). Stitch markers and holders.
Original yarn Tahki Cotton Classic (100% cotton; 1¾oz/50g, 108yds/100m)

Cardigan
Back
With smaller needles and MC, cast on 129 (141, 157, 169, 185) sts. Work 14 rows in Striped rib pat, inc 13 (15, 17, 17, 19) sts evenly across last row—142 (156, 174, 186, 204) sts. Change to larger needles. *Begin pats: Row 1 (RS)* Work 2 (0, 3, 0, 3) sts in rev St st, 0 (9, 0, 9, 0) sts in Seed st rib, [6 sts Chart A, 9 sts Seed st rib] 1 (1, 2, 2, 3) times, 20 sts Chart B, 9 sts Seed st rib, 6 sts Chart A, 9 sts Seed st rib, 20 sts Chart B, 9 sts Seed st rib, 6 sts Chart C, 9 sts Seed st rib, 20 sts Chart B, [9 sts Seed st rib, 6 sts Chart C] 1 (1, 2, 2, 3) times, 0 (9, 0, 9, 0) sts in Seed st rib, 2 (0, 3, 0, 3) sts in rev St st. Continue in pats as established until piece measures 14 (14½, 15, 16, 16)" from beginning, end with a WS row.
Shape armholes
Bind off 8 (8, 10, 12, 12) sts at beginning of next 2 rows—126 (140, 154, 162, 180) sts. Work even until armhole measures 8 (8½, 9, 9, 9½)", end with a WS row.
Shape neck
Next row (RS) Continue pat, work 40 (45, 51, 55, 61) sts, join a 2nd ball of yarn and bind off 46 (50, 52, 52, 58) sts, work to end. Working both sides at same time, bind off from each neck edge 2 sts once, 1 st once. Work even until armhole measures 9 (9½, 10, 10, 10½)". Place rem 37 (42, 48, 52, 58) sts each side on hold.

Right Front
With smaller needles and MC, cast on 55 (61, 69, 73, 81) sts. Work 14 rows in Striped rib pat, inc 14 (15, 16, 18, 19) sts evenly across last row—69 (76, 85, 91, 100) sts. Change to larger needles. *Begin pats: Row 1 (RS)* Work 2 sts in rev St st, [6 sts Chart C, 9 sts Seed st rib] twice, 20 sts Chart B, [9 sts Seed st rib, 6 sts

Chart C] 1 (1, 2, 2, 3) times, 0 (9, 0, 9, 0) sts in Seed st rib, 2 (0, 3, 0, 3) sts in rev St st. Continue in pats as established until piece measures same as back to armhole, end with a RS row.
Shape armhole
Next row (WS) Bind off 8 (8, 10, 12, 12) sts, work to end—61 (68, 75, 79, 88) sts. Work even until armhole measures 2 (2½, 2, 2, 2)", end with a WS row.
Shape neck
Dec 1 st at neck edge every row 9 (11, 11, 11, 13) times, then every other row 15 (15, 16, 16, 17) times. Work even until piece measures same as back to shoulders. Place rem 37 (42, 48, 52, 58) sts on hold.

Left Front
Work to correspond to right front, reversing shaping and pat placement, and replacing Chart C with Chart A.

Sleeves
With smaller needles and MC, cast on 53 (59, 63, 63, 65) sts. Work 14 rows in Striped rib pat, inc 13 (13, 13, 13, 15) sts evenly across last row—66 (72, 76, 76, 80) sts. Change to larger needles. *Begin pats: Row 1* (RS) K2 (1, 1, 1, 3), [p1, k3] 0 (1, 0, 0, 0) time, [p3, k3] 3 (3, 4, 4, 4) times, p3, work 20 sts Chart B, [p3, k3] 3 (4, 4, 4, 5) times, p3 (1, 3, 3, 0), k2 (1, 1, 1, 0). Continue in pats as established, AT SAME TIME, inc 1 st each side (working incs into Seed st rib inside 1 St st selvage each side) every 4th row 21 (20, 20, 16, 19) times, every 6th row 5 (7, 8, 12, 11) times—118 (126, 132, 132, 140) sts. Work even until piece measures 18 (19, 20, 21, 22)" from beginning. Bind off all sts.

Finishing
Block pieces. Join shoulder seams, using 3-needle bind-off. Place 7 (7, 7, 8, 8)

Back

Right Front

Sleeve

7 (7½, 8, 8, 8½)" 4¾ (5¾, 6½, 6¾, 7¾)"   4¾ (5¾, 6½, 6¾, 7¾)"   18 (19, 20, 20, 21)"

1"   9 (9½, 10, 10, 10½)"   7 (7, 8, 8, 8½)"

22 (23, 24, 25, 25½)"   12¾ (13¼, 13¾, 14¼, 14¾)"   16 (17, 17, 18, 18)"   16¾ (17¾, 18¾, 19¾, 20¾)"

1¼"   1¼"

19 (21, 23, 24½, 26¾)"   9¼ (10, 11¼, 12, 13)"   10 (11, 11½, 11½, 12)"

Cardigan Back Pat Arrangement

2 (0, 3, 0, 3) sts Rev St st	0 (9, 0, 9, 0) sts Seed st rib	6 sts Chart C	9 sts Seed st rib	20 sts Chart B	9 sts Seed st rib	6 sts Chart C	9 sts Seed st rib	20 sts Chart B	9 sts Seed st rib	6 sts Chart A	9 sts Seed st rib	20 sts Chart B	9 sts Seed st rib	6 sts Chart A	9 sts Seed st rib	0 (9, 0, 9, 0) sts Seed st rib	2 (0, 3, 0, 3) sts Rev St st

— 1 (1, 2, 2, 3)x —   — 1 (1, 2, 2, 3)x —

Cardigan Right Front Pat Arrangement

2 (0, 3, 0, 3) sts Rev St st	0 (9, 0, 9, 0) sts Seed st rib	6 sts Chart C	9 sts Seed st rib	20 sts Chart B	9 sts Seed st rib	6 sts Chart C	2 sts Rev St st

— 1 (1, 2, 2, 3)x —   — 2x —

Cardigan Left Front Pat Arrangement

2 sts Rev St st	6 sts Chart A	9 sts Seed st rib	20 sts Chart B	9 sts Seed st rib	6 sts Chart A	0 (9, 0, 9, 0) sts Seed st rib	2 (0, 3, 0, 3) sts Rev St st

— 2x —   — 1 (1, 2, 2, 3)x —

Cardigan Sleeve Pat Arrangement

1 st St st	22 (25, 27, 29) sts Seed st rib	20 sts Chart B	22 (25, 27, 29) sts Seed st rib	1 st St st

Vest Pat Arrangement

9 sts Seed st rib	6 sts Chart C	9 sts Seed st rib	20 sts Chart B	9 sts Seed st rib	6 sts Chart A	9 sts Seed st rib

— 4 (5, 6)x —   — 4 (5, 6)x —

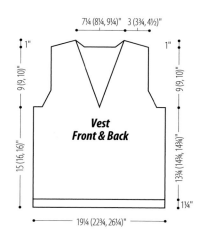

Vest Front & Back

7¼ (8¼, 9¼)"   3 (3¾, 4½)"
1"   1"
9 (9, 10)"   9 (9, 10)"
15 (16, 16)"   13¾ (14¾, 14¾)"
1¼"
19¼ (22¾, 26¼)"

Vest

Back

With smaller needles and MC, cast on 119 (141, 163) sts. Work 14 rows in Striped rib pat, inc 39 (47, 55) sts evenly across last row—158 (188, 218) sts. Change to larger needles. **Begin pats: Row 1 (RS)** Work [9 sts Seed st rib, 6 sts Chart A] 4 (5, 6) times, 9 sts Seed st rib, 20 sts Chart B, 9 sts Seed st rib, [6 sts Chart C, 9 sts Seed st rib] 4 (5, 6) times. Continue in pats as established until piece measures 15 (16, 16)" from beginning, end with a WS row.

Shape armholes

Bind off 12 sts at beginning of next 2 rows, 2 sts at beginning of next 10 (12, 16) rows, dec 1 st each side on next row, then every other row 3 (5, 5) times more—106 (128, 150) sts. Work even until armhole measures 9 (9, 10)", end with a WS row.

Shape shoulders and neck

Bind off 9 (11, 13) sts at beginning of next 4 rows, 8 (10, 12) sts at beginning of next 2 rows, AT SAME TIME, bind off center 48 (58, 68) sts for neck and, working both sides at same time, bind off from each neck edge 2 sts once, 1 st once.

Front

Work as for back until piece measures same as back to underarm, end with a WS row. Mark center 2 sts.

Shape armholes and V-neck

Shape armholes at side edges as for back, AT SAME TIME, place center 2 sts on hold for neck and, working both sides at same time with separate balls of yarn, dec 1 st at each neck edge every RS row 26 (31, 36) times. When armhole measures same as back to shoulder, shape shoulders as for back.

Finishing

Block pieces. Sew shoulder seams.

Neckband

With RS facing, circular needle and MC, begin at left shoulder and pick up and k76 (76, 82) sts along left neck, place marker (pm), k 2 sts from holder, pm, pick up and k76 (76, 82) sts along right neck, 60 (70, 80) sts along back neck—214 (224, 246) sts. Pm, join, shape V-neck and work pat simultaneously as follows: Dec 1 st each side of center front markers (ssk before and k2tog after markers) **every rnd including bind-off**, AT SAME TIME, work striped rib: **Rnds 1-3** With MC, *k1, p1; rep from * around. **Rnds 4-5** With A, k 1 rnd, then rib 1 rnd. **Rnds 6-9** Rep last 2 rnds with B, then with A. **Rnds 10-13** With MC, k 1 rnd, then rib 3 rnds. Bind off in rib.

Armbands

With RS facing, smaller needles and MC, pick up and k141 (141, 153) sts around armhole. Work rows 2-14 of Striped rib pat. Bind off in rib. Sew side seams, including armbands. ∩

---

markers along right front for buttonholes, the first at beginning of V-neck shaping, the last ½" from lower edge and 5 (5, 5, 6, 6) others spaced evenly between.

Front bands

With RS facing, circular needle and MC, begin at lower right front edge and pick up and k93 (97, 99, 103, 105) sts evenly along center front to beginning of V-neck shaping, place marker (pm), pick up and k1, pm, pick up and k159 (163, 167, 171, 175) sts to beginning of left front V-neck shaping, pm, pick up and k1, pm, complete to correspond to right front—347 (359, 367, 379, 387) sts. **Next row** (WS) Working row 2 of Striped rib pat, *rib to marker, k1, p1, k1 in next st; rep from * once more, rib to end. Work rows 3-14 of Striped rib pat and on row 7, begin 3-row buttonhole on right front at markers. Bind off in rib. Set in sleeves. Sew side and sleeve seams. Sew on buttons.

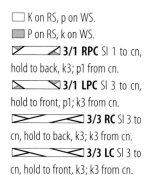

Chart A

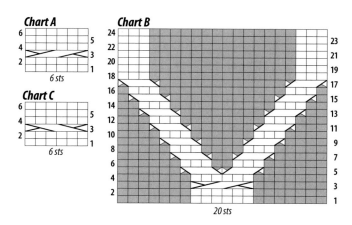

6 sts

Chart C

6 sts

Chart B

20 sts

☐ K on RS, p on WS.
▨ P on RS, k on WS.
⟋⟍ **3/1 RPC** Sl 1 to cn, hold to back, k3; p1 from cn.
⟍⟋ **3/1 LPC** Sl 3 to cn, hold to front, p1; k3 from cn.
⟋⟍ **3/3 RC** Sl 3 to cn, hold to back, k3; k3 from cn.
⟍⟋ **3/3 LC** Sl 3 to cn, hold to front, k3; k3 from cn.

The one question to ask in designing sweaters for work is: 'Will it be comfortable enough to wear for an 8-, 10-, or even a 12-hour workday?' Here is one that will.

This unisex vest is ideal for layering under a jacket. It's lightweight, non-restricting, and adds just the perfect warmth for chilly, winter mornings. The textured, all-over pattern appears more complicated than its actual 2 × 2 ribbing and simple rope cables.

The classic look and timeless styling is sure to become a versatile wardrobe basic—one that will make the transition to "after work" with ease and comfort.

Kathy Zimmerman

Wall Street cables

Notes
1 See *School* p. 102 for ssk and ssp.
2 When working underarm and neck shaping, work sts in St st if there are not enough sts to complete cable.

Skill Intermediate
Fit Standard
Sizes XS (S, M/L, 1X). Shown in Small.
Finished measurements 36 (41½, 47, 52)" around and 24 (25, 25½, 26)" long.
Gauge 36 sts and 32 rows to 10cm/ 4" over Chart A using larger needles.
Yarn 1250 (1500, 1735, 1960) yds. Light weight.
Needles Size 3.5 and 4mm/US 4 and 6, *or size to obtain gauge*.
Size 3.5mm/US 4 circular needle, 60cm/24".
Extras Cable needle (cn).
Stitch markers and holders.
Original yarn Skacel Collection Avanti (100% merino wool; 1¾ oz/ 50g; 137 yds/ 123m).

Back
With smaller needles, cast on 162 (186, 210, 234) sts. *Row 1* (RS) P2, *k2, p2; repeat from *. *Row 2* K2, *p2, k2; repeat from *. Work k2, p2 rib for 1¼", ending with a WS row.
Change to larger needles. *Begin Chart A & B pats: Row 1* (RS) P2 (0, 2, 0), work sts 11–24 of Chart A 0 (1, 0, 1) time, work 24 sts of Chart A 3 (3, 4, 4) times, work 14 sts of Chart B, p2, work 24 sts of Chart A 3 (3, 4, 4) times, work sts 1–12 of Chart A 0 (1, 0, 1) time. Continue in pats until piece measures 14½ (15, 15¼, 15½)" from beginning, end with a WS row.

Shape armholes
Continue pats, bind off 7 (9, 11, 13) sts at beginning of next 2 rows, 2 sts at beginning of next 16 (18, 18, 22) rows—116 (132, 152, 164) sts. Work even until armhole measures 8½ (9, 9¼, 9½)", end with a WS row.

Shape shoulders and neck
Bind off 7 (8, 10, 11) sts at beginning of next 8 rows, AT SAME TIME, bind off center 36 (42, 46, 50) sts for neck and, working both sides at same time, bind off from each neck edge 4 (5, 5, 5) sts once, then 4 sts twice.

Front
Work as for back until piece measures same length as back to underarm, end with a WS row. Mark center 2 sts.

Shape armholes and neck
Shape armholes as for back, AT SAME TIME, place center 2 sts on hold for neck and, working both sides at same time with separate skeins, dec 1 st at each neck edge every other row 24 (30, 33, 36) times, every 4th row 5 (3, 2, 1) times. When piece measures same length as back to shoulder, shape shoulders as for back.

Finishing
Block pieces. Sew shoulder seams.
Neckband
With RS facing and circular needle, begin at left shoulder and pick up and k70 (74, 74, 78) sts along left neck, pm, k2 sts from holder, pm, pick up and k70 (74, 74, 78) sts along right neck, 50 (54, 58, 62) sts along back neck—192 (204, 208, 220) sts. Pm, join and work in k2, p2 rib, working decs each side of center front sts as follows: Work to 2 sts before center sts, dec 1 (ssk if next st is a k, ssp if it is a p), k 2 center sts, dec 1 st (k2tog if next st is a k, p2tog if it is a p). Continue in rib pat until band measures 1", working dec before and after center sts on every rnd, including bind-off rnd.
Armbands
With RS facing and smaller needles, pick up and k150 (158, 158, 166) sts around armhole. *Row 1* P2, *k2, p2; repeat from * to end. *Row 2* K2, *p2, k2; repeat from *. Work k2, p2 for 1". Bind off in rib. Sew side seams, including armbands. ∩

6¾ (7½, 8, 8½)"   3 (3½, 4½, 5)"
1"   1"
8½ (9, 9¼, 9½)"
23 (24, 24½, 25)"
13¾ (13¾, 14, 14¼)"
Front & Back
1¼"
18 (20¾, 23½, 26)"

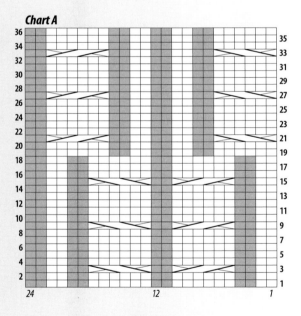

Chart A

24   12   1

Chart B

6
4
2
5
3
1
14 sts

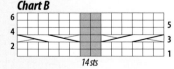

☐ K on RS, p on WS
▨ P on RS, k on WS
3/3 RC Slip 3 to cn, hold to back, k3; k3 from cn.
3/3 LC Slip 3 to cn, hold to front, k3; k3 from cn.

3-needle bind-off

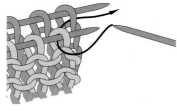

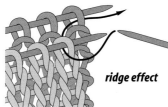

ridge effect

knitter's school

BIND-OFFS

3-needle bind-off *Uses* Instead of binding off shoulder stitches and sewing them together. With back stitches on one needle and front stitches on another, place *right sides together and wrong side facing.* *K2tog (1 from front needle and 1 from back needle). Rep from * once. Pass first stitch on right needle over 2nd stitch. Continue to k2tog (1 front stitch and 1 back stitch) and bind off across. *For a ridge effect* on the right side of the work, work as above but with wrong sides together and right side facing.

CAST-ONS

Cable cast-on *Uses* A cast-on that is useful when adding stitches within the work.
1 Make a slipknot on left needle.
2 Working into this knot's loop, knit a stitch and place it on left needle.
3 Insert right needle between the last 2 stitches. From this position, knit a stitch and place it on left needle. Repeat Step 3 for each additional stitch.

Invisible cast-on *Uses* As a temporary cast-on, when access to the bottom loops is needed: to knit, graft, attach a border, or for an elastic hem.
1 Knot working yarn to contrasting scrap yarn. With needle in right hand, hold knot in right hand. Tension both strands in left hand; separate the strands with fingers of the left hand. Yarn over with working yarn in front of scrap strand.
2 Holding scrap strand taut, pivot yarns and yarn over with working yarn in back of scrap strand.
3 Each yarn over forms a stitch. Alternate yarn over in front and in back of scrap strand for required number of stitches. For an even number, twist working yarn around scrap strand before knitting the first row. Later, untie knot, remove scrap strand, and arrange bottom loops on needle.

Long-tail or one-needle cast-on

Make a slip knot for the initial stitch, at a distance from the end of the yarn (about 1½" for each stitch to be cast on).
1 Arrange both ends of yarn in left hand as shown. Bring needle under front strand of thumb loop, up over front strand of index loop, catching it. . .
2 . . .and bringing it under the front of the thumb loop. Slip thumb out of loop, and use it to adjust tension on the new stitch. One stitch cast on.

Loop cast-on *Uses* To cast on a few stitches for a buttonhole.
Loops can slant either to the right or to the left. For right-slanting cast-on, work the next row through the back loop.

DECREASES

P2tog *Uses* A left-slanting single decrease.
1 Purl 2 stitches together. 2 stitches become one.

SK2P, sl1-k2tog-psso *Uses* A left-slanting double decrease.
1 Slip 1 stitch knitwise.
2 Knit next 2 stitches together.
3 Pass the slipped stitch over the k2tog.

Cable cast-on

Invisible cast-on

Long-tail or one-needle cast-on

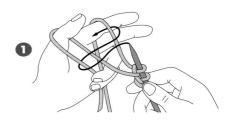

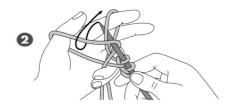

Loop cast-on

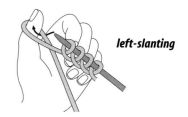

left-slanting

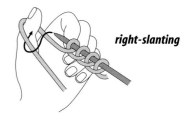

right-slanting

P2tog

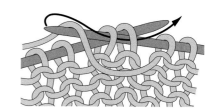

S2KP2, SSKP, sl2-k1-p2sso

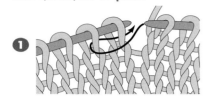

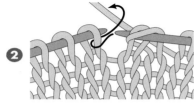

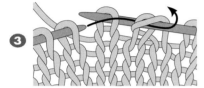

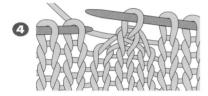

S2KP2, SSKP, sl2-k1-p2sso *Uses* A centered double decrease.

1 Slip 2 stitches together to right needle as if to knit.

2 Knit next stitch.

3 Pass 2 slipped stitches over knit stitch and off right needle.

4 Completed: 3 stitches become 1; the center stitch is on top.

ssk *Uses* A left-slanting single decrease.

1 Slip 2 stitches separately to right needle as if to knit.

2 Knit these 2 stitches together by slipping left needle into them from left to right. 2 stitches become one.

ssp *Uses* A left-slanting single decrease.

1 Slip 2 stitches separately to right needle as if to knit.

2 Slip these 2 stitches back onto left needle. Insert right needle through their 'back loops,' into the second stitch and then the first.

3 Purl them together.

sssk *Uses* A left-slanting double decrease.

Work same as ssk except:

1 Slip 3 stitches separately to right needle as if to knit.

2 Knit these 3 stitches together by slipping left needle into them from left to right. 3 stitches become one.

INCREASES
Lifted increase

If instructions don't specify, use right knit increase.

Knit

For a right increase: knit into right loop of stitch in row below next stitch on left needle (1), then knit stitch on needle (2).

For a left increase: knit one stitch, then knit into left loop of stitch in row below last stitch knitted (3).

Purl

For a right increase: purl into right loop of stitch in row below next stitch on left needle (1), then purl stitch on needle (2).

For a left increase: purl one stitch, then purl into left loop of stitch in row below last stitch purled (3).

Make 1 (M1, M1K) *Uses* A single increase.

1 *For a left-slanting increase (M1L):* with left needle from front of work, pick up strand between last stitch knitted and next stitch. Knit, twisting the strand by working into the loop at the back of the needle.

2 This is the completed increase.

3 *For a right-slanting increase (M1R):* with left needle from back of work, pick up strand between last stitch knitted and next stitch. Knit, twisting the strand by working into the loop at the front of the needle.

4 This is the completed increase.

Make 1 purl (M1P)

Occasionally instructions specify to work a Make 1 increase in purl.

For a left-slanting increase: Work as for Make 1, Step 1, except purl, twisting the strand by working into the loop at the back of the needle.

For a right-slanting increase: Work as for Make 1, Step 3, except purl.

ssk

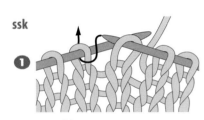

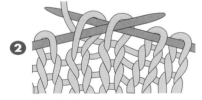

ssp

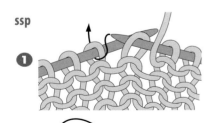

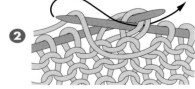

Lifted increase

 right knit increase RKI

 left knit increase LKI

 right purl increase RPI

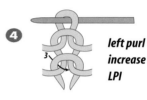 **left purl increase LPI**

Make 1

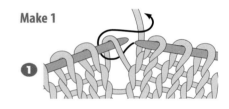

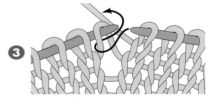

Backwards single crochet

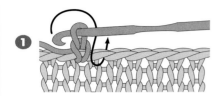

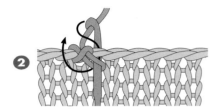

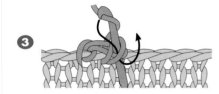

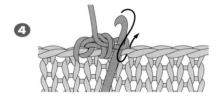

Grafting Stockinette

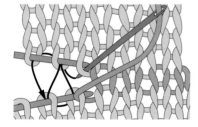

Grafting Garter st

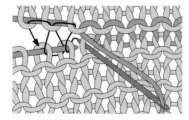

MISCELLANEOUS

3-row buttonhole

Uses For a buttonhole opening that runs perpendicular to the rows of the buttonhole band.
Row 1 Work 2tog, yarn over 3 times. *Row 2* Work into first yarn over, drop remaining 2 yarn overs.
Row 3 Work to buttonhole, knit into next stitch in the row below (into the yarn over).

Backwards single crochet

1 Work from left to right. **1a** Work a slip stitch to begin. **1b** Insert hook into next stitch to right.
2 Bring yarn through stitch only. As soon as hook clears the stitch, flip your wrist (and the hook).
There are now two loops on the hook, and the just-made loop is to the front of the hook (left
of the old loop).
3 Yarn over and through both loops on hook; one backward single crochet completed.
4 Continue working to right, repeating from Step 1b.

Grafting *Uses* An invisible method of joining knitting horizontally (row to row). Useful at tips
of mittens and hats, and for joining edgings together.

Stockinette graft

1 Arrange stitches on two needles.
2 Thread a blunt needle with matching yarn (approximately 1" per stitch).
3 Working from right to left, with right sides facing you, begin with steps 3a and 3b:
  3a Front needle: yarn through 1st stitch as if to purl, leave stitch on needle.
  3b Back needle: yarn through 1st stitch as if to knit, leave on.
4 Work 4a and 4b across:
  4a Front needle: through 1st stitch as if to knit, slip off needle: through next stitch as if to purl,
  leave on needle.
  4b Back needle: through 1st stitch as if to purl, slip off needle: through next stitch as if to knit,
  leave on needle.
5 Adjust tension to match rest of knitting.

Garter stitch graft

1 Arrange stitches on two needles so stitches on one needle come out of purl bumps (lower
needle) and stitches on the other needle come out of smooth knits (upper needle).
2–4 Work as for stockinette graft except: on 3b, go through the stitch as if to purl. On 4b, go
through 1st stitch as if to knit, and through next stitch as if to purl.

Knit through back loop (k1tbl)

To knit into the back of a stitch, insert the needle into the stitch from right to left.

Tassels

1 Wrap yarn around a piece of cardboard that is the desired length of the tassel. Thread a strand
of yarn, insert it through the cardboard and tie it at the top, leaving a long end to wrap around
the tassel.
2 Cut the lower edge to free the wrapped strands. Wrap the long end of the yarn around the upper
edge and insert the yarn into the top, as shown. Trim the strands.

Knit through back loop

Tassels

Wrapping sts on short rows

knit side

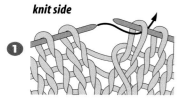

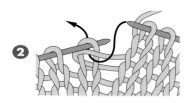

purl side

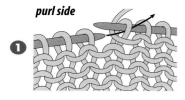

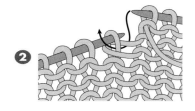

Yarn over before a knit

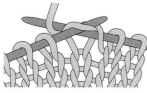

Yarn over before a purl

Wrapping stitches for short rows *Uses* Each short row adds two rows of knitting across a section of the work. Since the work is turned before completing a row, stitches must be wrapped at the turn to prevent holes. Work a wrap as follows:

Knit side
1 With yarn in back, slip next stitch as if to purl. Bring yarn to front of work and slip stitch back to left needle as shown. Turn work.
2 When you come to the wrap on the following knit row, make it less visible by knitting the wrap together with the stitch it wraps.

Purl side
1 With yarn in front, slip next stitch as if to purl. Bring yarn to back of work and slip stitch back to left needle as shown. Turn work.
2 When you come to the wrap on the following purl row, make it less visible by inserting right needle under wrap as shown, placing the wrap on the left needle, and purling it together with the stitch it wraps.

Yarn over

Before a knit
With yarn in front of needle, knit next stitch.

Before a purl
With yarn in front of needle, bring yarn over needle and to front again, purl next stitch.

Abbreviations
approx approximate(ly)
cn cable needle
cm centimeter(s)
dec decreas(e)(ed)(es)(ing)
dpn double-pointed needle(s)
est established
" inch(es)
inc increas(e)(ed)(es)(ing)
k knit(ting)(s)(ted)
LH left-hand
M1 Make 1
m meter(s)
mm millimeter(s)
ndl needle
oz ounce(s)
p purl(ed)(ing)(s)
pat(s) pattern(s)
pm place marker
psso pass slipped stitch(es) over
rem remain(s)(ing)
rep repeat(s)
rev reverse(d)
RH right-hand
RS right side(s)
rnd round(s)
sl slip(ped)(ping)
ssk slip, slip, knit 2tog
ssp slip, slip, purl 2tog
st(s) stitch(es)
St st stockinette stitch
tbl through back loop
tog together
WS wrong side(s)
wyib with yarn in back
wyif with yarn in front
yd(s) yard(s)
yo yarn over

Metrics
To convert inches to centimeters, multiply the inches by 2.5.
For example: 4" x 2.5 = 10cm

To convert feet to centimeters, multiply the feet by 30.48.
For example: 2' x 30.48 = 60.96cm

To convert yards to meters, multiply the yards by .9144.
For example: 4 yds x .9144 = 3.66m

Both simple and elaborate cable patterns use two basic techniques: the right cross (RC; also called the back cross) and the left cross (LC; also called the front cross)

2/2 Right Cross (RC)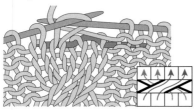

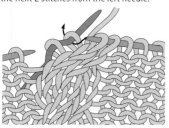

1 For a 2/2 RC (2 stitches crossing over 2 stitches and to the right), slip 2 stitches onto a cable needle and hold (let it hang) to back of the knitting. Knit the next 2 stitches from the left needle.

2 Then, holding the cable needle in your left hand, knit the 2 stitches from the cable needle. (See a completed 2/2 RC in the lower portion of drawing.)

2/2 Left Cross (LC)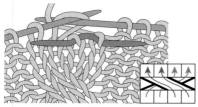

1 For a 2/2 LC (2 stitches crossing over 2 stitches and to the left), slip 2 stitches onto a cable needle and hold to front of the knitting. Knit the next 2 stitches from the left needle.

2 Then, holding the cable needle in your left hand, knit the 2 stitches from the cable needle. (See a completed 2/2 LC in the lower portion of drawing.)

Note The only difference in working a RC or LC is where you place the cable needle.

Cable patterns are just rearranged ribbings. Since most sweaters start with ribbing, we already know how to knit the knits and purl the purls. In a cable, every so many rows something else happens. Surely we can handle that.

Think back to when you first began to knit, the needles were the problem—and the solution. You had to learn how to hold and manipulate them, but they kept the stitches in order, presenting them one by one and in normal position.

Cables change that order. The cable needle (short and double-pointed) moves stitches off the knitting needle temporarily so that other stitches can be knit in their places. Charts show how many stitches to move and what to do with them.

cables & charts

Crossings can involve different numbers of stitches, can be repeated at different intervals, and can be combined in different ways. These differences result in an enormous range of cable patterns: double cables, diamonds, OXO cables, braids.

Keeping track

The basic mechanics of cables are few and simple. What are apparently complex are the patterns built from these crossings. Even more daunting are the panels combining several patterns that make up a typical Aran sweater. The challenge is keeping track of all these patterns—that means keeping track of what crossings to make where. A chart can really help with this.

The charts

A chart is a visual aid, a map, that communicates stitches as clearly as a clock does time. You may find that you only use the chart as a temporary help. Once you've knit a full repeat of the pattern, you have something even more valuable. Train yourself first to read the chart, then your knitting.

Other aids

Placing stitch markers between each pattern stitch (as shown by the Pat Arrangements) is very helpful, at least until the patterns develop and you can read a full repeat in your knitting. Use a magnetic row finder (a flexible magnetic strip and accompanying metal sheet) or a large sticky note to mark the relevant row on the chart (covering the row above the one you are knitting).

One at a time

Before attempting a multi-cabled design, try swatching each of the charts separately. Cast on the number of stitches on the chart plus 2 or 3 garter stitches at each edge. Work one or two repeats of the pattern. It will be much easier to begin the sweater when you have practiced the cables.

Twists

A crossing of 2 stitches (1/1) is called a twist and is not usually worked with a cable needle. Not surprisingly, there are R twists and L twists and several methods of working each. Just remember, if the key says 1/1 RT or 1/1 LT, you do not need to reach for a cable needle.

Working from charts

Charts are a graphic representation of knitting; they illustrate every stitch and the relationship between the stitches in rows.

Charts are graphs or grids of squares that represent knitted fabric, actually the right side of knitted fabric.

Squares contain knitting symbols.

The key defines each symbol as an operation to make a stitch or stitches.

The pattern provides any special instructions for using the chart(s) or the key.

The numbers along the sides of charts indicate the rows. A number on the right defines a right-side (RS) row, which is worked leftward from the number. A number on the left marks a wrong-side (WS) row that is worked rightward. Since many stitches are worked differently on wrong-side rows, the key will indicate that. In our example, the numbers for Charts A, B, and C are on the right and the pattern is worked circularly, but it would be no problem to knit back and forth in rows from the same chart. The odd-numbered rows of Charts A and C and the even-numbered rows of Chart B would be wrong-side rows (this keeps the cable crossings on right-side rows), and the key tells you what to do on the WS or the RS.

Bold lines within the graph represent repeats. These set off a group of stitches that are repeated across a row. You begin at the edge of a row or where the pattern indicates for the required size, work across to the second line, then repeat the stitches between the lines as many times as directed, and finish the row.

The sizes of a garment are often labeled with beginning and ending marks on the chart. This avoids having to chart each size separately.

Pat Arrangements Cabled sweaters often combine several cabled patterns, separated by a background pattern such as reverse stockinette or seed stitch. The Pat Arrangement presents this information for all sizes in a convenient visual form. Putting a stitch marker between each of the patterns can be a real help—at least until the knitting grows and you can read it.

yes, you can!

Chart A

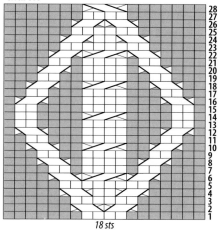

18 sts

Chart B

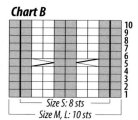

Size S: 8 sts
Size M, L: 10 sts

Chart C

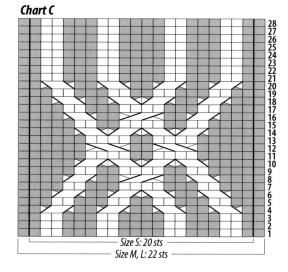

Size S: 20 sts
Size M, L: 22 sts

The charts and Pat Arrangement shown here are for the cover sweater (page 12).

☐ K on RS, p on WS

▨ P on RS, k on WS

2/1 RC Sl 1 to cn, hold to back, k2; k1 from cn.

2/1 LC Sl 2 to cn, hold to front, k1; k2 from cn.

2/1 RPC Sl 1 to cn, hold to back, k2; p1 from cn.

2/1 LPC Sl 2 to cn, hold to front, p1; k2 from cn.

2/2 RC Sl 2 to cn, hold to back, k2; k2 from cn.

2/2 LC Sl 2 to cn, hold to front, k2; k2 from cn.

2/2/2 RIB RC Sl 4 to cn, hold to front, k2, sl 2 p sts from cn to LH needle, move cn to back, p2; k2 from cn.

Body Pat Arrangement

0 (0, 5) sts Rev St st	0 (2, 2) sts 1/1 RT	8 (9, 9) sts Rev St st	2 sts 1/1 RT	18 sts Chart A	2 sts 1/1 RT	8 (10, 10) sts Chart B	2 sts 1/1 RT	20 (22, 22) sts Chart C	2 sts 1/1 RT	8 (10, 10) sts Chart B	2 sts 1/1 RT	18 sts Chart A	2 sts 1/1 RT	7 (9, 9) sts Rev St st	0 (0, 2) sts 1/1 RT	0 (0, 4) sts Rev St st

Yarn weight categories

	1 Super Fine	**2** Fine	**3** Light	**4** Medium	**5** Bulky	**6** Super Bulky
Also called	Sock Fingering Baby	Sport Baby	DK Light-Worsted	Worsted Afghan	Chunky Craft Aran	Bulky Roving Rug
Stockinette Stitch Gauge Range 10cm/4 inches	27 sts to 32 sts	23 sts to 26 sts	21 sts to 24 sts	16 sts to 20 sts	12 sts to 15 sts	6 sts to 11 sts
Recommended needle (metric)	2 mm to 3.25 mm	3.25 mm to 3.75 mm	3.75 mm to 4.5 mm	4.5 mm to 5.5 mm	5.5 mm to 8 mm	9 mm to 16 mm
Recommended needle (US)	1 to 3	3 to 5	5 to 7	7 to 9	9 to 11	13 to 19

Locate the Yarn Weight and Stockinette Stitch Gauge Range over 10cm to 4" on the chart. Compare that range with the information on the yarn label to find an appropriate yarn. These are guidelines only and reflect the most commonly used gauges and needle sizes for specific yarn categories.

Sizing Measure around the fullest part of your bust/chest to find your size.

Children	2	4	6	8	10
Actual chest	21"	23"	25"	26.5"	28"

Women	XXS	XS	Small	Medium	Large	1X	2X	3X
Actual bust	28"	30"	32–34"	36–38"	40–42"	44–46"	48–50"	52–54"

Men	Small	Medium	Large	1X	2X
Actual chest	34–36"	38–40"	42–44"	46–48"	50–52"

Fit Check Fit Category to see ease (additional width) built into pattern

Category	**Standard Fit**	**Loose Fit**	**Oversized**
Actual bust/chest +	2–4"	4–6"	6" or more